Learning a New Language

Learning a New Language

◆

Speech About Women and God

Beverly Jane Phillips

Dear Karen,
May God, She Who Is,
Continue to bless you in all the
ways you co-create with Her
Beverly Jane Phillips
7/12/09

iUniverse, Inc.
New York Lincoln Shanghai

Learning a New Language
Speech About Women and God

iUniverse books may be ordered through booksellers or by contacting:

iUniverse
2021 Pine Lake Road, Suite 100
Lincoln, NE 68512
www.iuniverse.com
1-800-Authors (1-800-288-4677)

ISBN-13: 978-0-595-36774-0 (pbk)
ISBN-13: 978-0-595-81192-2 (ebk)
ISBN-10: 0-595-36774-7 (pbk)
ISBN-10: 0-595-81192-2 (ebk)

Printed in the United States of America

Dedicated in loving memory to

my parents:

Dorothy Della Heeren Harvey

and

Alfred Mervin Harvey.

They taught me love of learning

and joy of work well done.

Contents

Preface

Many years of experience with women's circles in the church has taught me that there are for the most part two types of theological literature for women who want to study in order to deepen their faith and change their lives. One is the theology that says it is God-ordained that women are subordinate to men. When women in a church circle or study group are looking for a study to do together, this kind of theology usually comes in the form of a Bible study in which the students read passages of scripture and fill in blanks in a work book.

The other type is the academic work of feminist scholars who spend their lives digging deep into the history of women in the Bible, in theology, in church and in society and through their own spirituality reveal new ideas about God's intention for women, men, children and the creation as a whole. These works are life-changing, but very difficult and time-consuming to read. Women who live outside scholarly circles need to be exposed to these ideas so that they too can understand how much God values each one of them. One of the best of these books is *She Who Is, the Mystery of God in Feminist Theological Discourse* by Dr. Elizabeth A. Johnson. Her ideas touched me so deeply that I knew I had to share her profound theology and her eye-opening and heart-changing writing with women and men who have neither the time nor the confidence to read *She Who Is*. The result is this book.

My most profound thanks go to Dr. Johnson who taught me that it is right and healthy to call God by feminine names based on the fact that Genesis says that men and women are created in God's image. She presents facts and philosophies I had never heard before about how women have been portrayed and treated through the generations. In that process she changed not only my understanding of the Bible, of church history and of theology but she has also deepened my relationship to God, She Who Is. At the same time I must apologize to Dr. Johnson for any distortions of her theology or of the facts she presented in *She Who Is* that may be found in this book. Looking at her theology through the lens of my life and growth is bound to make it sound different, but I have tried hard to be faithful to her ideas. After all, these are the ideas and thoughts that have changed my life.

When I read a book I quite often skip over the thanks and acknowledgements, but now that I have written one I know how much a writer needs other people to be involved in the work. First, I want to thank the many people who knew I could do this before I was sure I could do it, among them Dr. Johnson herself who gave her approval and support of this idea when it was in a very fuzzy stage. Second, my thanks go to the She Who Is luncheon group from University Presbyterian Church in Tempe, Arizona who met with me every month for a year to talk about each chapter as it was being developed. Susan Hendrix who, at the beginning barely knew me, but wanted to learn more about what I was writing, called the group into existence. The other faithful friends and members of that group were Suzanne Brown, Kit English, Edna Fink, Louisa Starkey and Marcy Whittemore. Their discussion of my ideas and my writing was immeasurably helpful. Kate Wilmoth, director of the Resource Center of the Presbytery of Grand Canyon, offered me great encouragement after reading a very early version of the manuscript. Along the way I also relied on my daughter, Nancy Ann Baker, my daughter-in-law, Heather Phillips, and my sisters, Sharon Harvey, Margaret Morgan and Cynthia Rose Wolpert for critiques and support. Special thanks to Shirley Hipwell and Lorelei Hillman, good friends, who, in the last stages of getting the manuscript ready for publishing, unraveled long sentences, asked for clarification of some ideas and suggested punctuation where I had overlooked it.

I am equally grateful to the men who have played a part in the writing of this book. From the beginning Jim Phillips, my son, has been certain that the book would be written and published and so, in his way, pushed me to keep on. David Baker, my son-in-law, who is a creative writer and graphic artist not only gave me good advice on the publishing process but also designed the inviting cover for this book. The critique of three of the chapters which the Rev. Lyle Starkey so graciously and carefully did was of great help to me in restating some of the more difficult ideas. Last but certainly not least, I thank my husband, Norman! It is impossible to tell how much effect his sermons that I listened to almost every Sunday for over thirty years had on my feminist leanings but they most assuredly did because through all the years of his being a pastor and preacher he always lived and preached a Gospel of love and inclusion. Over the years of the writing of this book he has been a sounding board for new ideas and has been unfailing in his belief that I would accomplish this work and that it would be published. This is a much better book because when I thought it was finished he read the whole thing out loud to me! Together we found and corrected typos and grammatical errors, reworked long convoluted sentences and had lengthy and involved discussions about difficult concepts.

My thanks also go to all the unnamed people who knowingly or unknowingly contributed ideas and support to this book.

Beverly Jane Phillips
Gilbert, Arizona
July 26, 2005

Introduction

African violets filled the south window of my Grandma and Grandpa's dining room when I was a little girl. From that big window which looked out over the expansive Nebraska farmyard Grandma could see who was going by on the road or who was driving onto their place. She could see what part of his work Grandpa was doing as he moved from corn crib to hog shed to his tool shed or the barn. But equally as important, that window enabled her to have the greenest thumb with African violets of all the women in that part of the county.

Grandma must have had fifty violet plants on the shelves that Grandpa had built in front of the window. Even though there were so many of them she loved each one and gave each one the loving care it needed. She fed and watered them. She repotted and split them when they became too large for the pots in which she had planted them. She pruned them by removing the faded blossoms and the dead leaves.

Over the years I have come to believe that God is growing me much like Grandma grew her violets. On a daily and unfailing basis God has fed me, watered me and put me in places where I could grow as she[1] meant for me to grow. There have been extraordinary times when God pruned or repotted me that are clear and sharp in my memory as I think about my journey to this place of writing a book about naming God.

The first drastic repotting occurred when I was in college intending to become a children's librarian. My career plans changed dramatically during the summer between my junior and senior years when I served as a counselor at a junior high church camp. Speaking at the campfire on the closing night of camp, the dean, in his traditional talk, said that anyone could be a minister. In his words I heard God's voice calling me to be a minister. It was a shock to me because the denomination of which I was a member, the Presbyterian Church in the United States of America, had only the year before voted to allow the ordination of women to

---

1. Throughout this book I will be using masculine or feminine names and pronouns for God as the thought of what I am writing dictates. A close analysis of my choices may reveal that even in my use of inclusive language for God, I may be showing gender stereotypes. I, too, am a beginner at naming God with the new language.

the ministry. Being a shy person and uncomfortable among people there was no way I could see myself as a minister, let alone a pioneering woman minister. At first I laughed at the thought, thinking it would go away, but when it didn't I knew it was what I was being called to do. Like Grandma caring for her violets, God took me from one place and put me in another. I found myself with a completely different goal. It was a goal which was less expected and accepted for a woman than being a children's librarian, and one for which I felt ill-suited.

The second extraordinary time of pruning in my life was the removal of dead leaves of feelings of vengeance and even of hatred. In the middle sixties when sex education was thought by some to be a Communist plot, I was teaching the senior high class in the church of which my husband was the pastor. Having given the students a choice of several topics using the excellent curriculum prepared by our denomination I taught a series on sexuality in the Bible. Because of this series a small group of people in the church denounced my husband and me as Communists. These people cut themselves off from us in such a way that nothing was resolved and my feelings toward them became more and more resentful. After almost three years of harboring this bitterness, I realized my frame of mind was not hurting the people who had attacked us. It was hurting me by standing in the way of my own spiritual growth. Like my Grandma, removing useless leaves from her violets so they would be healthier, God removed the growth which was keeping me from being a spiritually healthy person.

The third noteworthy phase in my growth was a pruning away of dead blossoms. Jim, our son who is now thirty-eight years old, suffers from severe asthma which began when he was 18 months old. I spent agonizing hours in prayer as I held him or sat by his bedside while he struggled to breathe. My prayers did not take away Jim's asthma, however we did find a caring, innovative allergist who brought him much relief. Motivated by what I thought were unanswered prayers, I spent many hours during the summer of 1976 memorizing all the verses in the Bible which promise that prayer will be answered. The verses that were easiest to remember were the ones promising that whatever I asked for God would give me.

In September of that year, just before our daughter Nancy entered second grade, she was diagnosed with juvenile diabetes. During the hours of getting her to the hospital and having the initial tests done, I repeated my memorized Bible verses over and over feeling assured that since I was praying for her not to have diabetes the doctors must be wrong in saying she did. When the first IVs brought a natural rosy color to Nancy's ashen face I knew that she did indeed have Type I diabetes. Then I began to pray to God to take it away. Now, twenty-eight years later, she still has diabetes, but manages it well with the help of an insulin pump.

Just as Grandma removed what had once been beautiful flowers, God took away what had been beautiful ideas that had promoted my spiritual growth for a time but now were past their prime. In that pruning of me God was taking away the trite, easy answers to the mystery of God's work in my life and growing me into a life of the Spirit which has included writing my prayers in a journal every day. This practice of prayer has become a way of relating to God which is more than asking for things for myself or for my family and friends.

I don't for a minute believe that Jim's asthma or Nancy's diabetes and their subsequent life with these diseases is willed by God for my growth. But I do believe that God has used the sorrow and the continuing concern for our children as an opportunity to help me become more nearly the person she wants me to be.

The fourth extraordinary time in my life was a repotting which started years ago and is still in progress. Discovering that God is not male was truly an uprooting from an old pot and replanting in a new one. No one had specifically taught me that God was masculine. In fact, my pastors and teachers made it clear to me that God was not a sexual being. However, God was always referred to as "he." I was taught that God is a Spirit who is not male but still must be referred to as "he." The belief of Christianity that God came as a human being in the form of a man, Jesus, fortified the idea of God as male which has been in place at least since the Israelites formulated their faith in one God and one God alone as opposed to an array of gods and goddesses.

During the first forty some years of my life it never occurred to me that God could ever be referred to as any thing but "he." Using the masculine gender was better than calling him "it" since God is a personal God. What never occurred to me was that when we are restricted to calling God "he" we are saying to all women and to all men that it does make a difference what we call God. If it doesn't make a difference there shouldn't be any resistance to using feminine nouns and pronouns along with the masculine to name God. What was important, I believed, was not the nouns or the pronouns used to speak to the Holy One but that we speak to him. As a result I was unaware that people of many religions close God inside a very small box when they say that only masculine nouns and pronouns are appropriate to use when naming the Divine.

The move from using only male names for God to the possibility of also using feminine ones was a drastic repotting for me. It was accompanied by the realization that using masculine names exclusively gives men a higher status than women. At that point I also realized that not only was God portrayed as male, but that almost everyone of any importance whatsoever in the Bible was a man. The women mentioned in the Bible are few and mostly nameless, being used mainly for object lessons for such virtues as truth, honesty, faithfulness, and good works. Most often remembered and praised for a virtue they illustrated rather than any leadership they demonstrated, many of them remain unnamed and unimportant as real persons.

Not only were men the *active* subjects in the Bible stories, they were also the ones who were *addressed* in the sermons and prophecies of the Bible. As a woman, I could think that I was included with the men of these stories but the women of the day in which they were written were not included. Both Jewish religion and Roman society of New Testament times held women to be greatly inferior to men. In the Bible it seems apparent that masculinity is a more fitting attribute of the Divine than is femininity. None of this ever bothered me consciously until I read Elizabeth Dodson Gray's book, *Green Paradise Lost*, as part of the required reading for the Churchwide Gathering of Presbyterian Women at Purdue University in 1982.

Gray's ideas about the domination of men and the subordination of women bothered me. They bothered me so much I had a hard time reading the book all the way through. I was 46 years old and had been active in the church at least 41 of those years. I had never heard such radical ideas about God and about men and women. Somewhere in the course of my reading of the book I wrote inside the front cover: "What good does it do to know all of this? Christ is the ANSWER!" When I had finished reading it I wrote right below that note: "It's a great book!" That giant step for me opened up a whole new place to grow.

Reading Gray's description of the structure of power and importance in the world as a triangle set me thinking about things I had always accepted without question. She describes God as outside the triangle and at the top. Inside the triangle are layers: men at the top; under men are women; under women are children; under children are animals. Outside at the bottom is Nature. Before I read her book, it never occurred to me that this order of things was anything but the way God had planned it to be. In fact I had not thought about it very much. I had just accepted this view and lived with it.

Before I read Gray's book, it had never troubled me that the writing of history, philosophy, theology and literature through the generations that has been accepted as authoritative had been done almost exclusively by men. It never occurred to me that it was anything but natural that, with a few exceptions, everyone of any importance down through history was a man. Although few mountains, bridges or main streets are named after women I thought that was "natural" because men were the ones who did the things which were worth commemorating. The way history is told such women as Madame Curie and Florence

Nightingale were positive departures from what women are expected to be. If anyone had asked me about this predominance of men in history I probably would have said, "So what? That's the way it's supposed to be."

I was afraid as I read *Green Paradise Lost* 20 years ago. I knew from my own life experience and what I had been reading that there was truth in what Gray was saying. I was afraid of the conflict that having such thoughts, speaking such things could and probably would bring into my life with my husband, my father, my men friends at church and work and—even as strange as it is—with some of the women in my life.

In the last quarter of the 20th century, voicing the truths that I was coming to embrace was often called men-bashing. Betty Friedan's *The Feminine Mystique* and the "women's lib" movement that arose from it put many men and women so much at odds that anyone who sought equality for women and appreciation of women's abilities and accomplishments was viewed as a destroyer of marriage, family and home. One of the things I discovered early on in my reading of feminist literature was that the so-called "women's libbers" were neither the first ones nor the only ones in history to realize that women are equal to men. Nor are feminist theologians the first to realize that it is not sacrilegious to think of God in feminine terms. Those who fear and denigrate any movements to raise the status of women claim that using inclusive language for each other and for God is a result of "women's lib." Women's lib is often used as a synonym for feminism, but the two are not synonymous. Women's liberation is a movement for equal rights for women that began decades ago, but blazed in the 1970's. Feminism comes in many forms, but essentially it works toward freeing women from gender biases which have kept them from full equality with men and therefore from a full pursuit of their possibilities and goals.

It is outside the scope of this book to discuss the history of feminism except to say Jesus fit the description of a feminist in that he always valued women and treated them with dignity and respect as equals. Just one of many examples of feminists who followed Jesus' teachings is Julian of Norwich who in 1373 wrote her conviction that just as truly as God is our Father, so truly is God our Mother. Women and men theologians for centuries have been searching for meaningful ways to name God that recognize that we all—male and female—are created in God's image.

As I have discovered these men and women from the long ago past who believed and wrote that God's image is equally male and female, my self esteem and my appreciation of other women has grown wondrously. I have known, worked with, and taught many women who have fallen prey to the idea that feminism is the same thing as women's lib and that both are evils done by women who are too aggressive. Those who proclaim them evil are those who stand to lose power as women gain power in the gift of being women. It is of the utmost importance for the well-being of women, children, men and, not incidentally, of animals and plants, to shed light in these dark places which have always been held to be sacrosanct.

Men are victims of this same male dominated system which subordinates and oppresses women. William Pollack in his book, *Real Boys,* uses the term the "Boy Code" to describe the effect that generations of male domination has had on the boys of today. He contends that at the heart of the unease and suffering of boys today are outdated and highly dysfunctional gender stereotypes. These same gender stereotypes have imprisoned women in roles of inferiority which are defined by society. While the gender expectations for males involve strength and intelligence those expectations for females have been weakness and dependence. Since the characteristics assigned to women do not fit the male model of God, which is also based on gender stereotypes, believers have been prevented from naming God in ways that express the mystery and the fullness of God as both male and female.

Elizabeth Dodson Gray was the first one to open my eyes to the possibilities in feminist theology. Since then, through years of studying feminist theology and feminist Bible studies I have come to understand clearly that if I want God to continue to grow me I need to consider new and sometimes frightening ideas. Grandma repotted her violets—took them from pots that were too small and put them in pots that were larger so the plants could grow better. God has used Elizabeth Dodson Gray to "repot" me, to put me in a larger space so I could grow beyond where I had been.

In the 1980s, Christian feminist theologians began to advocate for the use of inclusive language for God. As much as the whole conversation about male dominance made sense to me, I still could not think that simply using masculine terms to name God had anything to do with a person's faith or the mission of the Church. Nor did I think that language for God had anything to do with the status of women or the deplorable conditions in which multitudes of the planet's people live. Even when I began to understand that calling God only "he" is making an idol of maleness I still couldn't use feminine names or pronouns for him for fear that I would offend "him". Especially in my daily prayer time there was a shadowy and fearful feeling that some how I was becoming a heretic.

In the process of caring for her violets, Grandma would carefully feed and water the ones she had repotted. Just so, God carefully fed and watered my growing awareness of what naming the Divine means. At age sixty one, I read Elizabeth A. Johnson's book, *She Who Is*. Dr. Johnson, more than any other Christian feminist theologian, has helped me see how important it is that women and men think seriously about what it means to name God. She uses the phrase "the name of God functions" to emphasize that whatever name we use for God gives God the human characteristics associated with that name. In turn what we call God summarizes and expresses our world view—the order we expect things to follow—and the resulting orientation of our lives and devotion. For centuries God has been described and addressed by male names only. Therefore maleness has been seen as superior to femaleness, a fact that makes men like God and women not like God.

While I was making these new discoveries through feminist theology I was afraid of what using feminine names for God might do to my position as an ordained Minister of Word and Sacrament in the Presbyterian Church (U.S.A.). In 1982, while reading *Green Paradise Lost*, I was afraid of losing the love and support of the men and women I loved and who I knew loved me. In the early 1990's in reading feminist theology I was afraid of losing my inheritance from the church I have always loved and the theology that, in spite of being always couched in masculine terms, helped me understand Jesus Christ as my Lord and Savior. Experiencing God as She Who Is, with Dr. Johnson's book as my guide, has shown me that I could think these radical new thoughts and grow in these new ways without losing my faith, but instead broadening and enriching it.

In *She Who Is* Dr. Johnson keeps the Scriptures and classical theology as the foundation of her faith, her thinking and her writing, even as she emphasizes how urgent it is for us to look at these two sources of our faith through the lens of women's experience. Some feminist theologians believe there is no hope in the Bible or in classical theology for a true understanding and acceptance of the value of women. Consequently they have left the Christian church and the Christian faith as well. In contrast, Dr. Johnson believes that there are legitimate ways to understand the writings of past generations, the Bible and classical theology that recognize the value of women as also being created in the image of God. If women are equal with men in being the image of God, then surely there must be the feminine in God. This recognition of God as being masculine and feminine and yet more than both has the potential to transform the whole order of things in society so that all people, male and female, child and adult, will enjoy a more humane way of life. At the same time such a theology will result in humans respecting and protecting creation. The idea that there is a hierarchy of which men are at the top and nature is at the bottom will be rendered obsolete and nature will be valued as a precious gift to be loved and protected.

She Who Is, a name for God that has Old Testament origins, has been working in the lives of women of faith in mysterious ways through all the generations even though she is always referred to as "he." With unfailing love and power, she has drawn women in all generations to herself in spite of the masculine language that portrays them as inferior. The same language contributes to the oppression of all people, men and women alike. Through generations of being told that the word "man" includes both men and women and that God isn't really male, women have still heard the message of love and power from She Who Is and have stayed in the church. Women have provided some of the best of what the church has said and done over the generations. In spite of being excluded from positions of leadership and influence by the use of male terminology women have stayed the course and have been not only part of, but also the cause of, great accomplishments in delivering the Good News to the whole world.

By her grace, through the years, God has led me to many places, many books and many people that have convinced me that we do more harm than good by continuing to label God strictly in masculine terms. As I read *She Who Is* I wanted everyone with whom I had ever discussed theology to know what I was learning. However the book is difficult to understand and requires a certain measure of knowledge about church history, theology, and the Bible. I knew most of the people I was thinking about would not read it even though I was recommending it every chance I got. So I have written this book in the hope of opening to others what Elizabeth A. Johnson opened to me: the possibility of naming God in ways that free men and women to experience the love of God who is Mother as much as Father.

My first idea of a way to spread her ideas was to write a paraphrase of her book, *She Who Is*. However, because of the extent of her scholarship, the depth of her faith, the scope of her concerns and the beauty of her writing it quickly became apparent that a paraphrase was impossible. After some struggles with format, I finally decided to work from my experience to what for me were the main ideas in each of the chapters in her book. Her faithfulness to Scripture fit well with my need to honor the Bible. Thus each chapter begins with an epigraph that includes a Scripture passage and a quote from Dr. Johnson which sets the stage for the ideas of the chapter. The text then begins with an example from my own experience which illustrates the topic of that chapter.

I make no claim to have presented Dr. Johnson's ideas in their entirety nor do I claim that I am representing her theology without fault or weakness. Much fervent prayer accompanied the writing of this book. My deepest desire has been to be as faithful as I could to her theology, which I believe is inspired by God. At the same time, I hope to open the hearts of people to the possibility of naming God in ways that allow women and men to experience the love and compassion of God who is Mother, Father and much more.

1

Language About God

To whom will you liken me and make me equal, and compare me that we may be alike?...for I am God and there is no other, I am God, and there is none like me. (Isaiah 46:5,9)

What is the right way to speak about God? This is a question of unsurpassed importance, for speech to and about the mystery that surrounds human life and the universe itself is a key activity of a community of faith. [1]

One night when I was a little girl, my father was tucking me into bed and talking to me about God. He said that God is a Spirit who is everywhere. I threw my arm out across the bed and said, "I've got my arm on him!" Daddy quickly corrected me saying, "No. God is Spirit. You can't put your arm on him but he is here with us all the time taking care of us and he is everywhere all the time." My parents, my grandparents and my church taught me that God is Spirit, Father, Love. By using these names for God they taught me how God acts. They taught me that God loves me like my father loved me. They taught me that God is with me always even though I cannot throw my arm across him. My loving Father God, because he is Spirit, is with me in ways that even my human father in all his love for me could not be.

These aren't the only names for God which I was taught but they were the ones that were emphasized and by which I tried to live. Some of my friends grew up in families and churches that emphasized other names for God. They were

---

1.   Elizabeth A. Johnson, *She Who Is, The Mystery of God in Feminist Theological Discourse,* (New York, Crossroad, 1996), 3.

taught that God is a strict father who demands obedience from his children, a judge who passes sentences on his people, and a king who rules his kingdom with an iron hand. Their emphasis was on God as a being of power and wrath whose main occupation is watching the behavior of people, judging them, and rewarding or punishing them according to how closely they follow the laws of his kingdom.

These three ways of naming God, father, judge and king, are not mutually exclusive nor does either one by itself define God completely. A loving father does expect his children to obey his rules and he does punish his children when it will be beneficial for them. The fact that God is called by all three of these names illustrates that one name for God is not enough. Our own personal experience of God shows that we experience the Divine differently in different situations.

What these three names for God have in common is that he is always "he". All assume that God is male. The importance of using names for God which include female names is not a whimsy of some radical thinking women who want equality for women. The importance of realizing that God's image includes both male and female is misunderstood and belittled. However, being able to speak of God with feminine names can have long term benefits not only for women but for children and men and all of creation. It is true for us as it has been for all people of all ages that how we refer to God sets the standard for our behavior. The standard that is set by using masculine names exclusively for God sets up a hierarchy in which men are more privileged than women, because when God is always "he" men are seen as more Godlike. In this hierarchy, women, children and nature are subject to men and all the rest of creation is subject to men. This arrangement needs to be changed if people and creation are to live in peace and wholeness.

> What is at stake is simultaneously the freeing of both women and men from debilitating reality models and social roles, the birthing of new forms of saving relationship to all of creation, and indeed the very viability of the Christian tradition for present and coming generations.[2]

Our speech about God glorifies God when it results in concern for the well-being of all people and of all nonhuman creation.

A currently popular motto found on a wide range of items in Christian book stores is "What Would Jesus Do?" For Christians, Jesus, who is God Incarnate, is the model for how we should act in specific situations in order to do the right thing and to bring glory to God. The answer to the "WWJD" question depends

---

2.   Ibid., 15.

on one's understanding of who Jesus is, and carries with it the understanding that a faithful person wants to act like Jesus/God acted. Who we believe God to be defines for us what is good behavior.

Any name used for God describes for human beings how God acts and what is important to God, thus showing us how we should act and what should be important to us. Jesus, who came to show the love of God, said that there is no greater commandment than: "You shall love the Lord your God with all your heart, and with all your soul, and with all your mind. This is the greatest and first commandment. And a second is like it, You shall love your neighbor as yourself" (Mt. 22:37ff). God who is Love shows us that at the very heart of believing in God is the act of love for God and for each other. As a consequence believers who see God as loving will see all people regardless of sex, sexual orientation, race, nationality, or creed as people to be loved, enjoyed and served. In society today, just as it was in Jesus' day, multitudes of people are degraded and mistreated. Among them are undocumented workers, welfare mothers, gays and lesbians, to name just a few. However much the world hates them, they are all loved by God who is Love. Churches and people who believe God is Love will serve these beloved of God. The God who is love shows us how to act.

God named Judge emphasizes that laws are of the highest importance with the resulting conviction that if God's laws are not rightly interpreted and strictly obeyed God will punish the offenders. When God is understood mainly by this name it becomes the duty of believers to obey and to insist that others obey in order for all to escape God's punishment. Undocumented workers are judged to be immoral breakers of the law who deserve punishment even though love and concern for their family's well-being may be the reasons for their illegal actions—they may be fleeing circumstances of extreme poverty. Single mothers are judged to be immoral because they have children with no father in the home. More than likely, they would dearly love to have a family that included the father of their children, but circumstances make it safer for them to live separately. Gay and lesbian people are judged to be immoral because they break the law that says marriage is between a man and woman only. No consideration is given to the possibility that deep and faithful love can characterize a same sex union in the same way it does a union between a man and a woman.

God is love and God is judge. God loves all people with a never ending, always forgiving love and is offended by any action that injures her beloved in any way. Therefore God does judge people whose actions hurt others. God does judge good and evil, but judging is not all God does. The names father, judge and king, are illustrative of how names for God affect our behavior, but there are many,

many other names, both masculine and feminine, that could be used. We need to use many names and both genders to describe God, realizing all the while that God is a mystery never to be fully understood or described.

Because we have a living God, whatever name we use for this Being acts as a verb carrying with it action. Even calling God a rock, an inanimate object, paints a picture of what God does. God who is a rock is solid and unmoving, a place to cling when all else is shaking. Whatever religion we belong to, naming God is one of the most important things we do as believers, as seekers, because that activity not only glorifies God but also sets standards for how individuals and society will act. A name for God causes things to happen between God and human beings, between human and nonhuman creatures, and between humans and the whole of creation. What we call God determines what is important to individuals and sets a standard for how society will act. The name of God functions. The name of God works. The name of God acts.

In Norse mythology Odin was the chief god of the people who came to be called Vikings. He was the god of art, culture, war and the dead but because he was worshipped mainly as a war god his followers were inspired to be warriors, the most ferocious of whom were called *Berserkers*. These warriors, who fought recklessly without armor and were said to feel "no wounds," terrorized Europe from late 700 C.E. until about 1100 C.E. Because Odin, their chief god, was cruel and merciless they were too. Like people of all ages and races what they saw in their god and believed about their god was considered by them to be the highest good. So for the Vikings the best a man could be was a fearless, merciless warrior like Odin. The name given to Odin functioned to make raiding and looting admirable activities. To say that the name of God functions is to say that what you call God is not only a way to address God, but also a way to live your life.

The Norsemen also had among their gods one named Frey, who was the god of agriculture and of fertility. His twin sister, Freyja, was the goddess of love and fertility. Odin is well enough known today that his name is often the answer to a crossword puzzle clue, but of Frey and Freyja little is known. If they had been the chief deities in the Norse pantheon, the history of Europe may have been different because then the highest good for the people would have been to be loving, peaceful, creative people.

The values individuals hold come from what they believe. As a result the values of a community, whether it is a family, a church, a town or a nation, come from the religious meanings which the members of that community adhere to. It may not be a group that would be described as religious, but what it holds as important is what is worshipped and what sets the standards for behavior for individuals within the community.

Bumper sticker slogans are oftentimes expressions of the values of a person or a society. One which is often seen on expensive pickup trucks and sports utility vans reads: "He who dies with the most toys wins." Most of us would not admit to wanting the most toys, but our homes and our spending habits show that even those of us who can't buy a lot of expensive "toys" still want them. The idea that one's happiness and value are determined by what one owns is widely held. So the standard for behavior of people in the United States is to work long, hard hours in order to have bigger paychecks in order to buy more things. People who earn small paychecks are shut out of buying the expensive items, but they are still deeply affected by the value that is placed on material things. It could be said in honesty that the name of God in the United States is Wealth and that this god is worshipped through the accumulation and protection of material goods. We name God from where we are, as have all the generations that preceded us.

We can create a god to be who we want god to be. Feminist theologians have been accused of wanting to create God in their own image as they work to show that feminine images describe God as authentically as masculine ones do. It is a strange charge to make in light of the centuries of God being described only in masculine terms, thus creating God in man's image. The goal of feminist theology, as we shall soon discuss, is not to replace male with female, but rather to understand that both are the image of God.

The women's movement of the last several decades is praised and blamed for many radical changes in our society. Among other things, it has been praised by many for opening up career choices for women and blamed by many for destroying the fabric of family life. Whether the opinion is positive or negative, it is impossible to deny that the women's movement has shed light on the fact that throughout the history of our country and other countries, women have been excluded from major leadership roles in religious hierarchies, business management and civil governing bodies where public symbols are created and public decisions are made. This has happened because male experience and abilities have been more valued than those of women. This denial of participation has placed women in a position of accepting, as though they were their own, symbols and decisions which are the product of the thinking and needs of men alone. Symbols that would show the value of women have not been considered. Decisions have been based on how the results will affect the lives of men, assuming that what is good for men is good for women. Excluding women from these affairs has resulted in the experience and imagination of women being subordinated to that of men.

Throughout the history of the world's religions which have embraced one God, that God has not only been the creator of all, the wisest of all, the strongest of all, the most powerful of all, but has also been almost exclusively described as masculine. Speaking of God as male has placed males above females and above all other parts of creation since maleness underlies all the other traits of God. If God-He is the best, the utmost, the highest then males must be as well. What it all boils down to is that since God is viewed as masculine all things masculine are godlike. How we got to this point is the substance of the following chapters, so suffice it to say here that this attitude has set up a world structure where women and children and nature have been subordinated to the will of men. Saying this always sounds like a condemnation of all men as though all men are domineering and conscious of their godlikeness to the extent that they take advantage of it. That is far from the case. One look at the world's structures of governments, religions, and economics reveals immediately that many men are also marginalized, subordinated and oppressed by this frame of reference. What we call God affects how we act and what is valued by society in general. In a world where all the decisions are based on the experience and needs of one half of the human population and the other half is ignored or debased there is imbalance in all of creation.

As a community of faith and the individuals within it speak to God they do need to have names for God. When two strangers meet and begin a conversation it is not long before they give each other their names if they feel happy and trustful in the new relationship and want to give it approval and possibly a lasting quality. God is Spirit, Divine Being, Ultimate Cause. We cannot know God from the inside of God's self so we need other names that are taken from our experience of God in our lives. What we call this Divine Being becomes the ultimate point of reference for understanding our experiences and the world. How we address God is an expression both of what we know and what we seek: the highest good, the most profound truth, the most appealing beauty. A community takes this goodness, truth and beauty and uses it to mold its identity and its practice.

In this task of naming God it can't be said too often that there is no one name to depict the great and mysterious God of the universe. Because there are no words that can describe God completely it is a good idea for us to speak of "naming toward God," as feminist thinker Mary Daly suggests.[3] In naming toward God we are acknowledging that we can never totally know this great and mysterious being who can never be fully described. Nevertheless, we must try if we want to know who God is, who we are, what the world is about and how all these are related.

For Christians, the Bible is the main source for understanding God and God's relationship to the world. Many feminists deny the value of the Bible because it is so obviously sexist and patriarchal in so many places and in so many ways. Reading the New Testament stresses the understanding of God as Father because it relies on the literalness of Jesus calling God Father and teaching us to use that name as well. Because Jesus called God Father that name became the best, the supreme name for God and made masculine pronouns a necessity. Jesus, in using the name Father, was not saying that God is only and exclusively a father. He was showing his disciples that he was intimate with God, saying, "I am God's son and that means that I can call him Daddy," which is the translation of the Aramaic word, "Abba." The word expresses an intimate relationship between Jesus and God, but it also carries with it a sense of God's compassion for all who suffer in any way.

What has been overlooked, and sadly so, in our reading of the Gospels is the fact that Jesus called God by many names other than Father. The idea of God's kingdom is profoundly central to Jesus' message, so speaking of God as a king is appropriate. (It should be noted that queens also rule kingdoms.) Jesus referred to God with many images. Dr. Johnson expresses this beautifully when she writes:

> Jesus' language about God is not monolithic but is diverse and colorful, as can be seen in the imaginative parables he spun out. A woman searching for her lost money, a shepherd looking for his lost sheep, a bakerwoman kneading dough, a traveling businessman, the wind that blows where it wills, the birth experience that delivers persons into new life, an employer offending workers by his generosity—these and many other human and cosmic instances are freely taken as metaphors for divine mystery in addition to the good and loving things that fathers do. God's way of dealing with human beings is at once like and not like all of these. Later Christian talk about God is poor indeed compared with the riot of images spun out in the Gospels' depiction of Jesus' speech.[4]

Even with this "riot of images" we should not stop calling God Father. All the traits that traditionally characterize a good father belong to God. He is a loving, strong provider and protector of us all. The actions of a good father are like the

---

3. Mary Daly, *Beyond God the Father: Toward a Philosophy of Women's Liberation* (Boston-Beacon, 1973)37ff.

4. Johnson, *She Who Is*, 80.

actions of God. However, we also know that God is not like the fathers that some children know who are domineering, self-centered and abusive. God is like a father. God is not like a father. God is more than a father.

The same thing would be true if we were to call God Mother exclusively. In these days of sensational TV talk shows we can see and hear women who are very domineering, abusive, cruel mothers so we know—possibly from our own experience as well—that not all mothers fit the stereotypical description of mothers as good, pure, patient, and wise. God is like a mother. God is not like a mother. God is more than a mother. We should not call God mother all the time any more than we should call God father all the time because neither name says it all. Nor does one gender describe God better than the other.

"God is God. It really doesn't matter what language we use for God so let's just keep calling him 'him'." This statement or one like it almost always comes up in discussions about the need to use inclusive language for God. The implication is that while God may be feminine as well as masculine the matter is not worth talking about. We call God Father but we really know that God is more than that name conveys. Further discussion contradicts what the Bible says and only obstructs a person's relationship to God. According to this logic we all know that God is more than masculine but we should continue to call him "he" because that is how we have always referred to Him. This way of thinking is itself an obstruction to faith. Putting God in this kind of box is a way of controlling who God is and what God does. The many and varied ways in which people, especially women, experience God are in a sense outlawed or at the very least relegated to unimportance. It follows naturally and inevitably that masculinity is elevated to being the one gender which is suitable to use to speak about God. This lays the foundation for placing men above the others in the family as well as in other societal structures.

So to whom shall we compare God? Who or what shall we say God is like? We cannot say with one word all there is to say about God. There is no one name that describes or encompasses this Holy Being. We need many names, both feminine and masculine, to describe the many activities of God and even then we will fall short of describing who God is in God's wholeness. We need to be aware that any name we choose for God applies to God only in its goodness.

Because the theme of the Kingdom of God is so central to Jesus' life and message, calling God "king" can bring deep meaning to faith and action. In the parables of Jesus, the kingdom of God is a place where the first shall be last, the hungry shall be fed and peace shall prevail. The kingdom Jesus describes is ruled over by a king who is compassionate, just, and wise. He is not like so many kings in the history of the world: arrogant, self-centered, greedy, brutal. In these contrasting statements about "king" we can see that God is more than a king. God is like a king. God is not like a king. God is more than a king. This way of thinking about names for God does not have its origins in current feminist thinking, but rather comes from early Christian theologians who wrote that speaking about God involves "a threefold motion of affirmation, negation and eminence."[5] This is a powerful formula that can keep us from putting God in a box by the names we use for her.

Human beings need to name God with many names for at least three reasons. First, we need to name God because every human heart senses and longs for someone or something greater than itself to worship. It has been said that in each heart there is a hole the size and shape of which only God can fill. People seek to have this longing fulfilled. In their innermost yearnings people who acknowledge that God exists want to pray, to have fellowship with God.

Secondly, God is involved in our communal lives. The prophet Isaiah describes the gods of the Babylonians as idols who have to be carried and who are so weighed down with the burdens of the people that they are incapable of saving even themselves (Is 46:2). In contrast to them, Isaiah quotes God describing himself as the one who carried and saved the people of Israel from their birth to their old age (Is 46:4). In the light of this contrast, God then asked what name Isaiah was going to call him, to whom he was going to make him (God) equal. In other words, God was asking Isaiah, "I have done and am doing such great things, things beyond your wildest imaginings. How can you name me? I am God and there is none like me."

Third, the God we name is a being who is more than we could ever describe in human language. As we open our minds to think creatively about names for God we see that God's many and varied activities present the possibility and the necessity of using many names for the One. World religions recognize this incomprehensibility of God. In the words of the Baghavad Gita, "God has a million faces." Hindu tradition says that God is one but he has a thousand names. The Muslim tradition offers a religious exercise in which the believer recites and meditates on ninety-nine of the most beautiful names for God. Whether or not it is accepted that these faiths are all speaking to the same God, it is universally acknowledged that there are many names for God.

The only way we humans can describe God, whose nature we cannot comprehend, is by using metaphors, by comparing this Unknown Being with something

---

5.   Ibid., 113.

or someone we do know. Quite often when a reporter asks a survivor of a tornado what it was like, the survivor answers that it sounded like a huge locomotive bearing down upon her. Most of us have heard a locomotive, but not a tornado. The witness uses something we know, a locomotive, to help us understand something we haven't experienced, a tornado. A tornado is like a locomotive, apparently, in noise but that word describes only one aspect of this kind of storm: the sound of this powerful force of nature.

Similarly, a name for God may describe one aspect of God's activity but does not describe the whole of God. There is no one person or one thing that God is like. As a person of faith engages in the daily work of relating to God, she comes to realize that there is no way to comprehend this God and yet she must keep trying to voice who this awesome, powerful, living mysterious being is to her.

Years ago J.B. Phillips, the British churchman, wrote a book titled *Your God Is Too Small.* This title describes clearly what we are talking about here. If we believe that God can be called by one name only then most certainly our God is too small. Looking back to the fourth century, Bishop Augustine of Hippo wrote that if you understand God then what you understand is not God. If we say there is only one way to speak about God then who we are speaking about is not God, but an invention of our own. We will have placed boundaries of our own making on God's being. Because the names we use for God have to be taken from what we know, there is a strong temptation to make God after our own image by choosing images which reflect who we are and what we value.

We have already heard Isaiah describe God as one who is so fully present with her people that she has borne her beloved from the womb and will carry them through life (Is 46:3-4). Isaiah not only paints a picture of God who is very intimate with people, but he also paints a stirring word picture of how mighty and exalted God is (Is 40). Isaiah proclaims that God is God in intimate ways in the lives of people and yet at the same time is the One who measured all the waters of the earth, marked off the heavens, weighed and measured the dust of the earth and the hills and the mountains. The Lord is supreme over all other beings and no one directed, instructed or taught him. Even as mighty as nations are they are like a drop from a bucket compared to God, says Isaiah (Is 40:15).

Indeed, after pondering what Isaiah has written about the Lord, how can we name him? What shall we call him? The prophet makes it clear to us that idols are totally insufficient since they are images "that cannot move." The Lord is most certainly One who moves. Isaiah speaks about goldsmiths making idols and that even after all the work the artisans put into creating these gods they are deaf and mute and unable to walk (46:5-9). It would be easy to name such a god as that because you can see it and feel it and touch it. You can place it where you want and it will stay there. No matter when you come back to it, no matter the circumstances in your life, every time you see an idol made with human hands you see the same thing. So you can give it a name. Call it Judy or Horace or Snail or anything you want to call it. It will always and in every circumstance be the same.

We can't call God one name to the exclusion of others. Over the centuries in the Christian church we have used names for God other than "Father," but they have been for the most part either masculine or neuter in gender. The result is that we have not made idols of wood or precious metals in order to worship them, but we have made an idol of words and devotion by always calling God "he," always calling God "Father." Indeed how can we name One who created the stars and called each one by name; who created the ends of the earth; who endures never growing faint or weary. At the same time this One tenderly holds all who wait for him so that they shall mount up with wings like eagles, run and not be weary, walk and not faint (Is 40:31).

> The prophet has described God's incomparable nature for a purpose, showing no interest in depicting God's transcendence for its own sake, in a vacuum, as it were. The insights offered into God's incomparable nature have led up to a clear statement of God's empowering nature. Thus is God's incomparable nature put at the service of God's love. The ones who were carried like babies held aloft on God's pinions, will be able to stand on their feet and come to God. In a descending image, from flying to running to walking, the chapter closes with a people capable of movement toward a God who is moving toward them.[6]

As we work at naming God we are moving toward the Great One who has first moved toward us.

God is mystery that cannot be solved. When we open our hearts to God by reading passages such as Isaiah 40:31 and as we experience God in our lives we know that God is beyond our ability to think or to say. Obviously, we can't relate to someone about whom we know nothing so we are compelled to compare God to what we experience in our lives; therefore this Holy Being must be named. God doesn't need to be named for God's sake, but rather for our sakes so that we as human beings can relate to God, and in our best efforts, live as God would have us live. What we call God is not so much a description of God as it is a way

---

6.   Johanna W.H. van Wijk-Bos, *Reimagining God, the Case for Scriptural Diversity*, (Louisville, Kentucky: John Knox Press, 1995), 19.

for us to connect with God in all the varying situations in which we, men and women, find ourselves. It is for the sake of an enriched faith that we must compare God not just to one half of his image but to the fullness of God's image, male and female.

As we contrast the idols to the God who is speaking in the Isaiah passages cited above we know the living, moving, hearing, speaking God. The God who has created this amazing, intricate, mysterious universe and all that is in it. The God who has created birds and butterflies of all colors, insects of amazing habits, trees and plants in such great variety that some of them have not yet been discovered! At one and the same time this awesome God wants to live with us! This mysterious and wonderful God wants to be part of our lives! The language we use in talking to and about God must be open to a variety of names and expressions suitable to God who cannot be contained by human thought.

2

Feminist Theology

Give her a share in the fruit of her hands, and let her works praise her in the city gates. (Proverbs 31:31)

In choosing the lens of women's flourishing to focus its thinking feminist theology takes the total personhood of women with utter seriousness, advocating women's well-being personally and corporately in all of these constitutive dimensions. [1]

The construction of sky scrapers in Chicago is an amazing process to watch! Whenever I was walking to or from my Bread for the World office or a meeting somewhere else, I always planned my route past such a construction site even if it was out of the way. Before any work was started on a new building the construction company would first build a wooden sidewalk with a roof at the edge of the street so that pedestrians could pass the site safely. On the street side, the board walk had a half wall so that there would be daylight on the walk, but on the construction side the wall was solid from ground to roof.

Knowing that people are naturally curious, the bosses in charge would drill peek holes in the inside wall at various places along the walk. Knowing also that people of various sizes and ages would want to see what was going on they drilled the holes at differing heights so that even a small child could peek in. Looking through several peek holes allowed a person to see different aspects of the work that was going on. But no one of them alone revealed the whole scene. Finally after months of vigorous activity during which the building rose into the air, the

---

1. Johnson, *She Who Is,* 31.

wooden sidewalk and the walls would be removed and the building revealed in its entirety.

For me, this became an allegory that was and still is helpful in my search for names for God which affirm my value and the value of all women. The rough wooden walls represent the veil of humanity through which we see God. The peek holes are the many, various ways humans see God at work in different ways in different times depending on the person's viewpoint. Like looking through the peek holes, our observations of God never give a full, complete view of God. Taking down the wooden walls and walk signifies the time which is to come which Paul describes with these words: "For now we see in a mirror dimly, but then face to face" (I Cor. 13:12). In some way unfathomable to us now, a new being will some day take the place of the finite human and we will see God in God's fullness and glory.

Through the centuries, human beings have been viewing God through little peek holes made by their personalities, their experiences and their time in history. Feminist theology provides new and authentic "peek holes" into God's nature and being. Since for generations men have been the acknowledged and acclaimed creators and thinkers, the ways we have been taught to view God have been those ways by which men see God. As men of power understood God only from their experience they insisted theirs were the only right and complete ways of naming God. Consequently women and their description of what they see through the peek holes of their experience have been left out almost entirely.

The flourishing of women can be likened to one of the peek holes, one of the ways of glimpsing God, that inspires Christian feminist theologians, both male and female, to name God in new and refreshing ways. Feminist theology looks at God from a position that makes the well-being and flourishing of women not only the starting point but also the goal of thinking about the mystery of God. It is the starting point as feminist theologians look at the condition of women all over the world today. The situation of women today may appear fairly good and acceptable if only women of certain colors, classes and countries are considered but when statistics about women worldwide are researched the picture is bleak. United Nations statistics show that:

- Women make up more than one-half of the world's population but they work two-thirds of the world's working hours.

- Women own one-tenth of the world's wealth and one-hundredth of the world's land.

- Three-fourths of the world's starving people are women and their dependent children.

- Women make up two-thirds of the world's people who are illiterate.

- "...more than one out of five women (22 percent) are victims of physical violence from an intimate partner in the United States. In Turkey that figure is 58 percent; in Kenya 42 percent; in Canada 29 percent; in Mexico, 27 percent...Worldwide, domestic violence is the leading cause of death among girls and women ages fourteen to forty-four."[2]

This list of shameful and disheartening facts could be much longer, but the point is that as feminists hear, read and experience these facts as reality, they are moved toward the goal of improving life for women everywhere. Suggesting the move toward a better life for women is not the same as demanding special favors or considerations, as some opponents of feminism would suggest when they speak about male backlash to the progress women are making. It is asking only that women's lives be given the same value as the lives of men. It is asking only that women's ideas and contributions in all areas of human life be appreciated and accepted as valid and worthwhile. However, the granting of such equality will involve huge changes in a system that has privileged men for generations.

Even in places where men's lives are poor, their women's lives are poorer. Even where men are considered deficient, their women are considered even more deficient. Feminist theology believes that when women's experience is given the same value as the experience of men conditions will improve for men as well as for women. One effective way to value women is to give them the right to a formal education that includes not only reading and writing but the possibilities of family planning and the skills that will prepare them to support themselves and their families. Time and experience have already shown that where women are valued enough to be educated their self-confidence increases and they are better able to provide for themselves and their children. No woman can thrive when she has so many children that her body weakens and she can't afford to feed, clothe and educate them. Statistics from the developing countries show that when women are taught that birth control is possible the number of children they bear decreases and their well-being and that of their children improves. The self-esteem and power that come with learning to read and to earn money are essential to the well-being of women. This flourishing of women wherever they live is the goal of feminist theologians.

---

2.   Anne M. Clifford, *Introducing Feminist Theology*, (Orbis, 2002), 15.

Concern for the well-being of women stems not only from the condition of women today but also from the demeaning of women in theology and practice that caused great suffering down through the ages. From time to time as I read of the low status of women that seems to be the norm in most cultures and most times, the thought has entered my mind that maybe women *are* inferior to men and can't take care of anything without the guidance of men. Perhaps because that belief is so widespread maybe it *is* true. However, wide acceptance of an idea does not make it true. We know from experience that the inferior position imposed on women is contrary to all that women are and do in their lives. The idea that women are inferior runs counter to the very truth of women's lives because history and experience show that women have creative power, dignity, strength and goodness which are inherent in their identity as human beings created in the image of God.

Theology always reflects the time, place and context of the theologians; thus when women seek to express how they see God from where they live they are doing what theologians throughout the ages have done. They are not seeking some special privileges or extra attention as claimed by those who cling to the patriarchal ideal that the way the world is currently structured with men in charge is the way it is supposed to be. Feminist theology results when women begin to look at their place in life, whether their suffering is great or small, and ask the question: "Did God, in creating male and female, intend for me and my sisters to be inferior to men and subject to them?"

Traditional speech about God would answer this question with a firm "Yes!" Looking at God and at the conditions around us in the attempt to provide an atmosphere in which women can flourish leads to sharp criticism of the traditional way in which we address God. One objection to any critique by feminists against traditional speech about God is that what women are pleading for only concerns women. In fact critical thinking about language for God is central to the whole faith tradition and is not diminished because it is women's newly found voices that are raising it. In the process of seeking the flourishing of women two ideals may be realized: a more peaceful and just order among human beings and more truth about the holy mystery of God.

Classical speech about God is oppressive and it makes an idol of maleness because it draws its concepts exclusively from the world of ruling men which says it is right for women, children and nonruling men to be subordinate. My computer automatically places a red line under the word "nonruling" indicating that there is no such word. Nevertheless, it is an accurate description of men who are also at the mercy of a system which gives power to the men who meet the commonly accepted standards for aggressiveness and acquisitiveness which have been established by society.

The oppressive nature of classical speech about God shows itself in the pattern of human relationships that put into practice the idea that if you are not a ruling man you are somehow deficient. Distinguishing between ruling and nonruling men underlines the fact that many men are treated as inferior and are denied opportunities just as women are. The ideal of manhood which is superior intelligence, aggressiveness, physical strength, and emotional noninvolvement discounts men who do not "live up to" these traits. Most feminist theology sees the liberation of men accompanying the achievements of women toward the goal that all people of both sexes will be equal in esteem and in opportunity. At the same time it must be said that even though they are considered less valuable than ruling men, nonruling men are still privileged because they consider themselves, and are considered by others, to be superior to women.

Idolatrous as well as oppressive are words that describe traditional speech about God. Idolatry results whenever we set a person, a thing, or an idea apart from and above all else and say it is the one model for all to follow without question. Thus, honoring male-dominant language as the only or even as the very best way of speaking about God becomes idolatry; it makes a single set of metaphors the only ones which can be used and limits the height and depth and breadth of the divine mystery. It is hard to accept these two words—oppressive and idolatrous—as descriptive of our names for God because all Christians everywhere, male and female, have been steeped in this language their entire lives. It is the language of Christian worship. It is the language of Christian education. It is the language of Christian hearts.

The discussion of the oppression of women, children, nonruling men and creation, and of the idolatry of making God male, sets the stage for defining in simple ways the ideas of patriarchy and hierarchy. Patriarchy is the belief system that says it is right and proper that men should hold a position of control over all the rest of creation including women and children. Because men embody the characteristics of God-He they should be in charge of all things and determine the course of all events. This logic leads to hierarchy which says that since some people are seen to be more valuable than others they are higher up on the ladder of importance than those others. These are the patterns of dominance and subordination which produce violence and suffering in families, nations and the world.

In spite of the male-centered language that has denied their value and caused them so much suffering, women through the ages have embraced the Christian faith, working tirelessly for the church. Most have survived with a deep spiritual relationship with God and an abiding love for the Church. Such an unlikely result in the face of such treatment can only be a gift given by the love and mercy and grace of God who created male and female equal, who understands from her own being what it means to be a woman.

Under the impact of historical changes in economics, governance, world relations and family life for the last two centuries, speech about God has become more debatable. The doctrine of God which the church has inherited has been in the process of reformulation for some time. In response, feminist theology has been generating new language by looking at the ancient texts and at contemporary experience together, weaving them together in ways that restore the place of woman as being in the image of God. Because the experience of women is receiving more attention these days, women's voices are being heard in discussions of how to think in our times about an ancient God.

The concept of God which has come under attack has been that which is identified as classical *theism*. Dr. Johnson sums up theism with these words:

> It signifies the understanding that there is God (contrary to atheism), that God is one (contrary to polytheism) and that the one God is not to be identified with the world (contrary to pantheism).[3]

As theism took shape through medieval, especially Protestant and Roman Catholic thought, under the influence of the rational nature of the Enlightenment, it came to describe God as a Being separate from the Trinity. The result was that God came to be seen as the Supreme Being who made all things and then removed himself from his creation. This Supreme Being, if he (theism always refers to God in male terms) is to be supreme, must be essentially unrelated to the world and must be unaffected by it. The joy or sorrow, grief or happiness, well-being or suffering of his creatures can not affect him lest they would change him and thus erase his supremacy.

In theory, theism claims that the mystery of God is beyond all ideas and metaphors, but in practice it models God after the role of a reigning monarch. While claiming that God cannot be described, theologians of medieval and early modern times set in concrete a certain image of God. Adjectives used to describe God are those which portrayed the opposites of human traits: infinite, eternal, unchangeable, perfect, all-knowing, all-powerful. All these descriptions served to set God above and apart from his creation. In this way infinite mystery was

---

3.   Johnson, *She Who Is*, 19.

reduced to an independent Supreme Being alongside other beings, but greater in all ways than any and all others.

The idea of God being separate, far off and above all, results in questioning the necessity, or even advisability, of believing in God. Among the questioners are atheists who reject such a God because they claim, among other things, that religion based on this God is an opiate to keep suffering, oppressed people satisfied with their lot in life. Other groups protest theism on the grounds that this God allows such terrible suffering when with his power and might he could put an end to the evils that cause suffering. The fact that he stands by and allows such misery to befall his creation labels him cruel and uncaring.

The list of questions goes on as we hear the voice of the poor criticizing a theistic God who appears neutral about their suffering but seems to favor unjust civil and church rule. Additional questions center on the validity of making a Supreme Being so anthropocentric, so manlike, as Western Christianity learns more about Eastern religions. In response to these questions and accusations, theologians are struggling to find other ways of speaking about God that will show God as one who is connected with humans and with all of creation. Their efforts are leading to conversation, based on Scripture and experience, about God who liberates people; God who is incarnated in human beings; God who relates to creation; God who suffers with creation; God who is hidden and unknown. It is at this stage of the breakdown of classical theism that feminist theology speaks from women's experience with fresh language about the mystery of God.

In any area of human endeavor whenever anything new is suggested, the old must be defined and its shortcomings highlighted. Therefore feminist theology begins by defining sexism and its effects not only on women but on the whole of creation. At the heart of defining sexism is historical study of the development of attitudes toward females that have led to the belief and practice that women are inferior. From the study of the historical basis of sexism, including the Bible, Christian theologians who are feminist move to the proclamation that women's experience is valuable and appropriate for thinking about and naming God.

Sexism may be defined briefly as the belief that persons are superior or inferior to one another on the basis of their sex. Clearly, when God himself is seen to have only the characteristics of the male half of the human race, the other half, described as lacking those masculine qualities will be seen as inferior. Not only are women believed to be inferior because they lack the "masculine" qualities, but so are men who don't measure up to the standards of masculinity. The problem does not lie in the use of male metaphors for God because men too are made in the image of God and the experience of men is truly appropriate to name toward

God. The problem exists because the male terms are used exclusively, literally and patriarchally. There are many names for God in the Bible (and in lesser known sources) that are not masculine, but they are overshadowed and unused because of prevailing Christian language for God. Feminist theology searches for and uncovers these buried treasures.

The testimony of Scripture is that the mystery of God is beyond the ability of humans to comprehend. Yet it is accepted and defended that God is literally "he." The fact that when feminine images are introduced there is such loud objection proves the claim that the masculinity of God is taken literally. In addition, seeing God as a powerful monarch, a result of the theistic idea that God is a Supreme Being enthroned on high above his kingdom, sets the stage and makes the conditions right for God to rule over all and for men who are godlike to have the same right to rule. Logically, in this way of thinking, the fact that God sent his son to redeem the world adds weight to the idea of man as ruler over all. Since God became human in the man Jesus, there must be more divine qualities in men than in women.

As was said in the first chapter of this book, the idea of God "functions." It is not just an idea held in the minds of humans. Patriarchal God language sets the world stage for the drama in which social structures in family, church and society are ruled by men. If God who is male rules with a mighty, all-powerful hand, then it is acceptable and even natural for men to rule just as completely. This implies that men alone are the image of God and that women and, therefore, women's qualities and attributes are deficient and are ultimately the symbol for all evil. "If God is male, then the male is God," is Mary Daly's stark statement to describe this situation.[4]

The effect on women of patriarchal ways of referring to God is devastating to women's religious identity, to their sense of dignity and to their sense of power and self-esteem. This expected and accepted arrangement of the world's social structures has destructive effects in the lives of women not only in the physical ways already listed with statistics, but unavoidably on their self worth.

For a girl child her secondary status in the world becomes part of her life at a young age, whether she lives in a culture that teaches her her place in subtle ways or in a culture where she is blatantly used as a servant to her father and brothers and eventually to her husband. Through the years the girl who has been subtly kept down may rise above it or deny her subordination just as society denies it. Or she may buy into the idea that she is truly inferior to her men friends or hus-

---

4.   Daly, *Beyond God the Father*, 19.

band, and consider that it is a good thing because it is the way God intended things to be. Girls who are treated as property by the men in their lives may escape by fleeing or, like the girls subtly discriminated against, accept inferiority as their own and give in to it. Another more dangerous option is that, at the risk of their lives they may stand up for themselves and for other women.

God, named and described by classical theism, is the perfect example of the solitary, ruling male ego. The connection between God described as male and sexism is emphasized by feminist theologians. When theology looks at its tradition of exclusivity in the light of the experience of the "other half" of the human race then ideas about God and names for God will require a new language that expresses the newness and the unsuspected depths of this inclusive way of speaking about God. The naming of God which has been done in the past, and is still being done in some theologies, leaves women on the outside looking in. The human reality of women wherever and whoever they are can provide suitable metaphors for the holy mystery of who God is.

Discontent with the patriarchal way of seeing God and the world lies heavy on the hearts of women and of some men but how does a person speak it? Thinking and speaking of God using inclusive words and metaphors is akin to learning a new language. New words must be learned and used. Old words must be used in new ways. This is an emotional as well as an intellectual activity. Learning and using these new words is difficult even for people who believe it is high time we acknowledge that the flourishing of women, and thereby the flourishing of men, children and creation, depends upon the inclusion of women in the naming of God and in all other ways as equal in value with men.

3

The Image of God

o o o o o o o o o o o o o o o o o o o o o o o o o o o o o o o o o o

So God created humankind in his image, in the image of God he created them; male and female he created them. (Genesis 1:27)

The mystery of God is properly understood as neither male nor female but transcends both in an unimaginable way. But insofar as God creates both male and female in the divine image and is the course of the perfections of both, either can equally well be used as a metaphor to point to the divine mystery [1]

"A mighty fortress is our God, a bulwark never failing." Martin Luther in 1529 wrote the words and the tune to this hymn which is still an all time favorite with Christian worshippers all over the world not just in Lutheran churches but in churches of many denominations. It is a hymn that stirs the soul and thrills the heart as it describes in towering words and tones God's strength and steadfastness in the persons of God, Son and Spirit. The strength of God continues in the second line as well when it says "Our helper He amid the flood of mortal ills, prevailing."

These words express what we have experienced about God. We know that God is as strong as a mighty fortress and as a bulwark in our lives, God never fails us in our battle against the evils that assail us daily. But as meaningful and moving as these words are no one who sings this song then pictures God as a great gray castle with turrets and towers made of huge boulders and mortar like the cas-

---

1. Johnson, *She Who Is,* 55.

tles and fortresses seen in parts of Europe to this day. Nor do we think, when we call God a bulwark, that he is a defensive wall made of earth, rocks and logs. Everyone knows these words are metaphors, which we use to help us understand that God who is strong and unwavering will protect us. Luther goes on in the second line to give us another picture of God—God as our helper in the midst of "mortal ills." The words of the hymn are dramatic though somewhat outdated for people in the twenty-first century; however the power of the metaphors remains. Luther did what all humans must do in speaking about God. He used metaphors.

Whatever name we use for God is a metaphor. According to Webster, a metaphor is "a figure of speech containing an implied comparison in which a word or phrase which is ordinarily and primarily used of one thing is applied to another." Speaking metaphorically is the act of finding a similarity between two things one of which is better known to us than the other and then using the better known word as a way of describing the lesser known. When we want to speak about God who is mysterious and always beyond our understanding or describing we have to use words that we know and understand. These words are based on our own experience.

Carol M. Bechtel, in the study for the Kerygma Series, *Hallelujah, The Bible and Handel's Messiah,* contrasts the power of metaphor with the dullness of language without metaphor. She wrote that one of the characteristics of the lament Psalms is that they use vivid metaphorical language.

> Psalm 22:6, for instance, rivets our attention with its claim, "But I am a worm, and not human…" Such language is infinitely more powerful than any flat description of the psalmist's emotions. Imagine, if you will, the same verse translated into the jargon of modern psychoanalysis: "I am suffering from low self-esteem and am having difficulty reaching my full human potential." The language loses quite a lot in the translation. Metaphors enable us to say what we mean, only more so. By commandeering the sights, smells, and sounds which our senses associate with these vivid word pictures, they force us into a far richer experience of what is being described. They 'give us a taste,' as it were, of the psalmist's own experience.[2]

Thinking about who God is requires that we use metaphors because our human minds cannot comprehend who this Being is. Despite the danger of taking a metaphor literally there is no other way to speak about God. Thus, in nam-

---

2.   Carol Bechtel, *Hallelujah, The Bible and Handel's Messiah,* (Pittsburgh, PA, The Kerygma Program, 1995), 58.

ing God by something we know we are able to understand something about God who is unknowable.

Metaphors used by writers of the Bible to describe God are not limited to masculine ones, but are also feminine and neuter. Biblical metaphors liken God to father, king, warrior, judge and other roles which are generally expected to be masculine. They also speak of Spirit, mother hen, mother bear, a woman searching for a lost coin and others to describe God with feminine characteristics while such Biblical metaphors as rock and door imply no gender. Even so, for generations and generations the pronouns that have been used are always, almost without fail, masculine. If we believe the passage from Genesis to be true which states God created us in the Divine image, "male and female", it should be acceptable, and even commonplace, to use names such as mother, queen, sister, aunt or other feminine metaphors for God, as well as to use feminine pronouns.

The use of only the masculine when speaking of the Divine is not a decree from God. Rather it is because of cultural stereotypes of gender that we use only masculine names and pronouns for God.

> This is not to say that there are no differences between women and men, but it is to question the justification of the distribution of virtues and attributes and to find it less than compelling as a description of reality. Such stereotyping serves the genuine humanity of neither women nor men, and feeds an anthropological dualism almost impossible to overcome.[3]

Sex and gender are terms that are often used interchangeably but they do have distinct meanings. *Sex* refers to the physical aspects of a human being which are genetically determined, while *gender* is the term used to refer to characteristics assigned to individuals by the culture in which they were born. There are obviously physical differences between male and female, but both equally reflect the image of God and are to be enjoyed and celebrated because they are God's design for the creatures made in her image.

The belief that some groups hold regarding the Bible is that it was written when God literally took the hand of a writer and moved it across the pages writing down each word, each sentence, and each paragraph. In this view what we have in the Bible is without doubt or debate the actual words of God. It is the truth as it happened. If this is the truth then the inferior position women have been given is God's idea from the beginning of creation and therefore should be unquestioned and unchanged.

---

3.   Johnson, *She Who Is,* 49.

An alternative view of the inspiration of the Scripture is that God did indeed inspire the writing of the Scriptures. God did it not by mechanically moving the hands of the writers, but by being so active in their lives that they were inspired to write the truth about God as they experienced it. People who accept the first view, the literal one, tend to believe that Moses himself wrote the first five books of the Bible. However, based on knowledge gained over two centuries of intensive study by Biblical scholars trained in the languages, history and archaeology of the region, it is now understood that Genesis, along with Exodus, Leviticus, Numbers, and Deuteronomy, was passed along as oral tradition and then put into writing at various times by various people. If we date Abraham and Sarah at about 1800 B.C.E. and fix the setting of the canon of the Hebrew Bible toward the end of the first century C.E., we can see that this whole process of passing on the Hebrew Scriptures, what we are used to calling the Old Testament, took the better part of 2000 years.

The book of Genesis was written and/or edited by at least four different individuals or groups designated by historians and Biblical scholars as the Jahwist (J) which was the earliest source and was from the time of the monarchy about 950 B.C.E.; the Elohist (E) from the Northern monarchy about 750 B.C.E.; the Deuteronomist (D) from the Southern Kingdom about 650 B.C.E. or later; and the Priestly (P) from the period after the fall of the nation in 587 B.C.E.

"J" and "E" are so named because "J" uses the name "Yahweh" ("J" comes from the German "Jahwist") and "E" uses the name Elohim when referring to God. The designation "D" is given to parts of the narrative related to the ideas in the book of Deuteronomy. The strand labeled "P" takes its name from the fact that it conveys priestly interests such as ritual matters. The strand referred to as "J" is the source of two of the formative ideas about gender in the Bible.

There are two stories of creation in Genesis. The story in the first chapter was written by "P" and the story in the second chapter by "J." In Genesis 2:21-22, we read that woman was created from man, which has been interpreted to mean that the woman is inferior to the man, since she was created second and from a piece of man.

Since the story told in Genesis 2 is the more familiar of the two creation stories, we need only to summarize by saying that in this story, written by "J," God created Adam and then created all the other creatures in the search for one that would be worthy and able to be the helpmate of the man creature. When none of those created ones seemed right for Adam, God put him to sleep, took a rib from his side and made a woman. Whether the writer of this version of the story meant it intentionally or unintentionally, it still remains that what he wrote conveyed the idea that male humanity has superiority over female humanity. Woman's place is further diminished by the story in Genesis 3, also written by "J" which is the story of the fall. Here we are told that the woman was the one who gave in to the tempting of the serpent and thereby was the cause of sin and evil in what before had been a perfect place. It is "J" who

> ...takes us into a patriarchal world in which men place themselves at the center of society (indeed at the center of creation) and in which women (as well as beasts and birds) exist for man's support.[4]

In a brave and beautiful attempt to raise the status of women, a 17th century feminist, Rachel Speght, an English clergyman's daughter, observed that woman was created from refined matter, while Adam was created from dust. She went on to say that woman was not made from Adam's foot, to be his low inferior nor from his head to be his superior, but from his side, near his heart to be his equal. This attempt to explain away the perceived second class place of women has become popular on plaques and other items in some Christian book stores. However comforting it may be for today's woman, it is inadequate as a slogan for changing the status of women because it focuses on Genesis 2:21 to the exclusion of Genesis 1:27.

The creation story placed first in chapter one of Genesis is identified as being from the strand labeled "P" and probably was written in about 587 B.C.E., 300 years after the "J" strand. In it we read that God created humankind in his own image. He created them male and female.

> Without establishing relative rank or worth of the genders, the spinner of this creation tale indicates that humankind is found in two varieties, the male and the female, and this humanity in its complementarity is a reflection of the deity. For feminist readers of scriptures, no more interesting and telegraphic comment exists on the nature of being human and on the nature of God. The male aspect and the female aspect implicitly are part of the first human and a reflection of the Creator.[5]

The two together reflect the one image of God not solely in their sexuality; but they also reflect the image of God together in their creativity, imagination,

---

4.   Denise Lardner Carmody, *Biblical Woman, Contemporary Reflections on Scriptural Texts*, (New York, Crossroad), 11.

5.   Carol A. Newsom and Sharon H. Ringe, eds., *The Women's Bible Commentary* (Louisville, Westminster/John Knox, 1992), 12.

and ability to reason. Together they are given gifts that show God's nature so that, like God, they can lavish care and protection on the creation as well as to use it for their own sustenance.

The "P" source doesn't have a story in which the first couple are tempted to disobey God, but "J" does. "J" couples the creation story in Genesis 2, in which woman is created from man, with the story found in Genesis 3 which is the temptation and fall story. The story of Eve and the serpent serves to reinforce the idea of female inferiority and adds to it the belief that women are by nature evil. In this story, Eve is the temptress—the one who led Adam astray. Her giving in to the tempter's beguiling offer of a taste of the fruit of the tree of the knowledge of good and evil caused them to be exiled from Eden and subsequently, according to some theologies, caused all the evil in the world forever. Because of Eve all women ever since have had pain in child birth and men have been under the sentence of hard labor, or so the story goes. Eve caused the fall of humankind from the perfect conditions in the Garden of Eden to the hard conditions of the world outside the gates of paradise. As a result she and her sisters through the ages have had to bear that shame and guilt.

Today's society generally accepts in some vague way that the creation and fall stories are ancient, that they may be mythical and that they need to be reinterpreted, but the ideas and beliefs they engendered are still prevalent in the world as our masculine language for God bears out. These ancient ideas that, not only is male superior to female, but also that male is more righteous than female form the background for male only language for God. Because God can be neither inferior nor unrighteous any words associated with women who are thought to be both inferior and unrighteous are unfit to use to name God. Discussions of feminine metaphors for God may cause tempers to flare and judgments to rage because these ideas from Genesis are so inbred into the thinking of people everywhere. Lest only the Bible, Christians and Jews be blamed for all of this, it must be said that other religions have similar stories and similar beliefs about the status of women.

This was the culture in which Jesus grew to manhood and lived as an adult, but he never accepted or practiced the idea that any person was inferior to another. In his eyes and in his heart even a leper was valued as much as a healthy person, a prostitute as much as a righteous man. The religion and society in which he grew up taught that women were not only inferior but that they were unclean. An every day prayer of a Jewish man was "thank God I am not a woman." In contradiction to laws and mores that said a man should not talk to a woman who was not his wife nor should he touch or be touched by a woman who was not his wife, Jesus talked to women and taught women publicly. He let women touch him. He ate with women. In his teaching he even used different roles of women as metaphors for God.

> Jesus alone among the men in the gospel record did not accept the first-century mold for women. He took women as seriously as he took men. He never patronized women or demeaned them or constricted them to "their place" as defined by the social conventions of his day. He rejected stereotyping women as "birth vessels" or kitchen helpers. He used female images for God and for himself, and he chose as his metaphor for conversion women's unclean birth process; "being born anew" or again.[6]

Even though the word had not been coined in Jesus' time, we can still say that Jesus was a feminist! He saw that women were smart, capable, strong and loyal. He knew the value of women and believed they should flourish. He appointed women as apostles, a fact that has been completely overlooked in history, in Bible study and sermons. Jesus won as an apostle the Samaritan woman at the well (John 4:7-42). She is the *first person* to whom Jesus reveals himself as the Messiah, resulting in her going out and telling other people about him with such power that they also believed that he was the Messiah. The word "apostle" means someone who has been sent out to preach, to proclaim the Good News of the Gospel and that is certainly what she did, bringing her whole village to believe in Jesus as the Messiah.

The women at the empty tomb on Easter morning were also apostles. In each of the Synoptic Gospels, Jesus is quoted as commissioning them to go out and tell what they have seen. He did not accept the model of inferiority and uncleanness of women that the society of his time lived by. Jesus knew that women could understand, speak, lead, and be courageous. He knew that they could qualify to be bearers of the Good News.

Whether or not women in the church of the first century were called apostles is not clear because for the last 1000 years the church has taught that only men were apostles. As women scholars dig ever deeper into history and previously unknown or neglected texts, it is being revealed that women did serve in the role of apostles. For example, in Romans 16:7 Paul writes of a person named Junias who was a prominent apostle before Paul was. There is an ambiguity in Paul's Greek in this passage, so that by 1200 C.E. the Church—unable to imagine a

---

6.   Elizabeth Dodson Gray, *Sunday School Manifesto, In the Image of her?* (Wellesly, Massachusetts, Roundtable Press, 1994) 36.

woman as an apostle—substituted the male form of the female name Junia even though no such name for a man is recorded anywhere else. Recent scholarship has discovered in other documents that there was a woman apostle named Junia who lived during this time In the 1500s Martin Luther, in his commentary on Romans, assumed that this apostle must be a man, leaving no room for the possibility of women apostles and adding strength to the argument that women should not be priests or ministers.

Luther and other reformers and theologians found a firm foundation in the Bible for their claims that the "natural" inferiority of women should exclude them from ritual functions and from teaching and preaching. The Apostle Paul laid that foundation in the letters he wrote to the early churches. Some of his writings can be attributed to disciples of his who came later, but in the letter to the Corinthians, generally accepted by biblical scholars as being his words, he stated clearly the inferiority of woman.

> For a man ought not to have his head veiled, since he is the image and reflection of God; but woman is the reflection of man. Indeed, man was not made from woman, but woman from man. Neither was man created for the sake of woman, but woman for the sake of man (I Cor 11:7-9).

The use of exclusively masculine names for God came from a culture that put into practice the belief that women are inferior to men. They reasoned that God must be male, because he could not be what women were considered to be: weak, passive, manipulative, evil, unclean. Based on this reading and interpretation of scripture held in place by religious and social patriarchy, Western theologians perpetuated and legitimatized these ideas. Like Paul they wrote beautiful, coherent, resounding statements about the nature of God and Christ which are central to the Christian faith to this day but, like Paul, for all intents and purposes they shut women out of being made in the image of God.

The early church fathers were also influenced by the Greek philosopher Aristotle (384-322 B.C.E.) who said that a human being is born female because of the lack of certain qualities and that there is a natural defectiveness in females that makes them misbegotten males. In other words women are the victims of birth defects. If all human beings were born perfect they would all be men. This idea is as illogical as the widespread practice in India and China today of aborting girl babies because it is more desirable to have boy children. The logical conclusion of such ideas and practices is that the day would come when no babies would be born since there would be no women to bear them.

One of the fathers of the church, Tertullian, who lived from 160-230 C.E., addressed this message to women, blaming them for the death of Christ:

> Do you not realize that you are each an Eve? The curse of God on this sex of yours lives on even in our times. Guilty, you must bear its hardship. You are the devil's gateway; you desecrated the fatal tree; you first betrayed the law of God; you softened up with your cajoling words the one against whom the devil could not prevail by force. All too easily you destroyed the image of God, Adam. You are the one who deserved death, and yet it was the Son of God who had to die.[7]

Augustine, (354-430 C.E.), Bishop of Hippo in North Africa, believed that men are superior to women because that is the very nature of things:

> Woman does not possess the image of God in herself, but only when taken together with the male who is her head, so that the whole substance is one image. But when she is assigned the role as helpmate, a function that pertains to her alone, then she is not the image of God. But as far as the man is concerned, he is by himself alone the image of God just as fully and completely as when he and the woman are joined together into one.[8]

The idea of the inferiority of women was so pervasive and so deep seated that in 585 C.E., nine centuries after the death of Aristotle, a general church council was called in France which debated among other things the topic, "Are women human and fully person?" Sixty-three bishops and representatives of bishops debated and took a vote. By that vote it was declared that women are fully human.

Thomas Aquinas (1225-1274 C.E.), echoing Aristotle, taught that there is a basic principle that every active element creates something like itself which means only men should actually be born from copulation because men are the active agent and women are passive. The energy in semen aims of itself to produce something equally perfect, namely another man. He accepts Aristotle's biology which holds that it is from an unfavorable circumstance such as a damp, south wind blowing on the night of conception that a baby girl is born. Aquinas, while not believing that women are the slaves of men, did believe in accordance with his times that they are inferior.

---

7.   Elizabeth A. Johnson, *Consider Jesus, Waves of Renewal in Christology,* (New York, Crossroad, 2000) 101.

8.   Ibid., 101.

Statements like these about women would not be made in a more scientifically developed and open-minded society such as ours, but these are the men (Aristotle, Tertullian, Aquinas and their heirs) who laid the foundation for our religious life as it exists in the West today and thereby for our secular life. These are the ideas and thoughts that have set the stage for the subordination and oppression of women worldwide even in what we Westerners would consider more enlightened times and societies. In the light of such writings it would be unthinkable to call God by feminine names or to use feminine pronouns for God.

The influence of these early teachers, clergymen, and philosophers, has lived on in attitudes toward women down through the ages. The inferior place assigned to half the population of the world has caused untold injury to women, children and creation itself. It has set the stage for seeing people in a hierarchical order. When some are considered superior then it follows that the inferior ones should be excluded from all kinds of rights such as education, voting and property holding. In the case of nature which is at the bottom of the triangle of importance it becomes acceptable to plunder its riches for the use of human beings.

Language used for God reflects the values of the people doing the describing, the naming. In the case of male only names for God, a vicious cycle exists in which men are the ones who do the naming and thereby the masculine becomes predominant because the predominant ones have the power to name. The names used for God have to be masculine because males, who are seen to be more like God than women are, rule. It is true, there have been ruling women in some times and places, but they are few and far between and in some cases even go unrecognized in the telling of history. There is a clear call today for inclusive language about God that comes from a culture that has begun to acknowledge that women are equal to men; that women are not the cause of all sin and evil in the world; that women are capable of rational thinking and acting; that women can make valuable contributions to the world both inside and outside the home. The realization is dawning that God should not be represented only by maleness, as this not only hints at but teaches dogmatically that God is male and therefore to be male is closer to the Divine perfection and authority.

Neither one nor the other, neither male nor female, should be left out of God talk. We should not change our language about God to use only feminine names and pronouns for God because we would then make men inferior and women superior. Nor should we declare that male and female are the same for that would erase the great variety, diversity and uniqueness which the two different sexes exhibit. We need a new model which will recognize and proclaim that since male and female are created in the image of God they are of equal value. In this new model we will also celebrate the differences between male and female as signs of the creativeness and imagination of God.

The accusation is leveled at women who speak of God in feminine terms that they are creating God in their own image; that women are trying to make God into a woman. In reality what feminist theologians, men and women, are struggling to do is to reshape language in such a way that the nature of God can be shown in those who are made in the image of God male and female. If the destructive idea that some are superior and others inferior can be erased the world will operate in such a way that all parts of God's creation will be seen as good and valuable and will be treated equally. The harmony which will result will allow the flourishing not only of women, but of men, children and all parts of nonhuman creation.

The problem is not that male names are used for God, but that they are used exclusively and literally. Men are made in the image of God and their experience does provide meaningful metaphors for God, but they are not the only, the complete way to speak of God. Women are also made in the image of God and their experience also provides meaningful metaphors for God. All names for God are subject to the formula: God is...God is not...God is more than...Applying the formula using the name "mother" we must say: God is like a human mother in all her goodness. God is not like a human mother who is cruel or uncaring. God is more than a human mother. Any name we use for God fits this formula. Nothing that we call God, no name that we give God, changes who God is. Naming God with a multitude of names, male and female, can only deepen our relationship with God and bring about the kind of world that will please and glorify her.

4

Women's Experience

○ ○

As many of you as were baptized into Christ have clothed yourselves with Christ. There is no longer Jew or Greek, there is no longer slave or free, there is no longer male and female; for you are all one in Christ Jesus. (Galatians 3:27,28)

…Greek philosophical tradition equates the male principle with spirit, with mind and reason, and most importantly with act, reserving for the female principle a contrasting identification with matter, with the inferior body and passion, and most importantly with potency. In this profoundly dualistic world view, male is to female as autonomy is to dependence, as strength is to weakness, as fullness is to emptiness, as dynamism is to stasis, as good is to evil. [1]

"Let him win!" That was the advice given to me and to most girls who were teenagers in the 1950's. The same advice was given to young women in the years before that and has been in the years since. When a boy asked you to go bowling or to play miniature golf on a date you were supposed to let him win. If you didn't, he wouldn't like you and wouldn't ask you out again. If you got into a discussion on any topic and you knew as much or more about it than he did you were supposed to let him think he knew more than you did. We were supposed to keep our intelligence hidden because we were taught by our mothers, our teachers and even our friends that boys don't like girls who are too smart.

---

1.   Johnson, *She Who Is*, 35.

I bought this advice lock, stock and barrel. Even as I grew into adulthood, if a man with whom I was conversing said something that I knew was inaccurate, even though I was certain I knew better, I would not only keep quiet, but even more damaging to me, accept that he must be right! If a man contradicted something I said or believed I immediately felt sure that I must be the one who was in error. Having accepted the generations-old idea that men are more intelligent than women, I sat silently on the sidelines in many discussions and situations. I thought that was the way God meant it to be.

Scarlett O'Hara, in *Gone With the Wind*, expresses her frustration, indeed her anger, at having to be what in her society she, as a woman, was expected to be.

> I'm tired of everlastingly being unnatural and never doing anything I want to do. I'm tired of acting like I don't eat more than a bird and walking when I want to run, and saying I feel faint after a waltz, when I could dance for two days and never get tired. I'm tired of saying "how wonderful you are" to fool men who haven't got one-half the sense I've got, and I'm tired of pretending I don't know anything so men can tell me things and feel important while they're doing it.[2]

Even though this story is about life during the Civil War, the restrictions that were put upon women in those days still rest upon women today. The prevalence of eating disorders and the way girls drop out of competitive sports at an early age testify to the fact that women are still constricted by the expectations of society. Many women and girls, like Scarlett, are tired of something, but they can't put a name to it and are, in fact, afraid even to try to name it, for fear of unknown and probably negative results in their relationships with men and boys in their lives.

Not only did I view myself as inferior to men—less intelligent and not as brave—but I believed that was true about all other women as well. I knew I was smart and able while at the same time believing that boys and men were smarter and more able. Because I accepted this ideas as true about myself, I also believed it to be true of others. I was put down and in turn I put other women down. There was a time in my early adult years when I even preferred the conversation of men because of the perception that women's talk was trivial. Women's talk is still often described as "idle chatter" or "gossip." The characteristics attributed to women through the ages have denied the personhood and worth of women. Shedding this way of thinking about myself and about other women has been part of a process that is like my Grandma pruning her violets. She would look

---

2.   Margaret Mitchell, *Gone with the Wind* (Macmillan, 1945) 79.

over each plant and remove the dead blossoms and leaves. God has been and still is removing the thoughts and feelings that I have always harbored about my own inferiority and that of other women.

During the heyday of "women's lib," in the 1960s and 1970s, I had a friend who was truly obnoxious in her constant talk about how women are and always had been oppressed and subordinated. I knew what she was saying was true, but that truth, in my mind, paled in comparison with the oppression and cruelty suffered by both male and female people of color. What has become clear to me through my study of feminist theology is that she and I both had valid insights about the issue which cannot be separated into sexism and racism. The concept that women are inferior makes possible the subjugation of any people, male or female, white or colored, rich or poor and of nature as well. The belief that women are inferior can be extended to include anyone who does not have the qualifications of a ruling male, resulting in their subjugation. Placing women in an inferior role affects not only women but also men, races, religions, and nature because it gives birth to the idea of relative worth, of hierarchy. If some are always of greater importance, then others are always of lesser importance. If some are deemed more fit to rule and make decisions, then others must be subject to their rule and not be part of decision making.

> In society women have for most of history been denied political, economic, legal and educational rights—in no country in the world are these yet equal to men in practice. In situations where people suffer intolerably from poverty and racism, the dynamic of sexism burdens women with added and profound exploitation: they are the underclass that functions as "slaves of slaves," subordinated to men who themselves are already oppressed…. To make a dark picture even bleaker, women are bodily and sexually exploited, physically abused, raped, battered, and murdered. The indisputable fact is that men do this to women in a way that women do not do to men. Sexism is rampant on a global scale.[3]

The inferiority of women has been accepted as fact for so long that it seems God-given from the very beginning of creation, but in reality it is rooted in writings from ancient times. The Greek philosophical tradition taught gender dualism very clearly. Greek thinkers framed the idea of spirit as being that which is good and matter as that which is evil. Men were identified with spirit, mind, and reason, which was seen to be good; and women with matter, bodiliness and emotion which were seen to be evil. There was, and still is in some ways and in some

---

3.   Johnson, *She Who Is,* 25.

places, a lingering belief that women are the symbol of evil. This identification of women with evil, while not openly verbalized in our society is witnessed to by the quickness with which people judge a woman who has been raped about how she was dressed, the time of day and where she was when the rape occurred. This concept of women as embodying evil contributes significantly to the opposition to using feminine names for God.

The idea of the superiority of men and the inferiority of women has become such a firm foundation of our description of who men are and who women are that women have come to internalize these images, to believe them to be true of themselves. Male-centered language and symbol systems have shaped and continue to shape women and their image of themselves. An important thing for women of the Judeo-Christian faith to understand is that this is not the way the whole Bible presents women even though men have interpreted it that way for generations and women have accepted it for generations.

Dr. Johnson makes the point that women are the image of God when they exercise stewardship over the earth in their capacity to rule with ecological care as representatives of God; in their intelligence and their ability to reason; in their freedom which is suitable for union with God; in their creativity, their sociality, their community with each other and with men, children, and the whole earth; in their physical being; in their destiny.

> The wholeness of women's reality is affirmed as created by God and blessed with the identity of being in the divine image and likeness. Practically speaking, this leads to the moral imperative of respect for women, to the responsibility not to deface the living image of God but to promote it through transformative praxis. In linguistic terms it offers basic justification for speech about God in female symbols, since women themselves are theomorphic. If women are created in the image of God, without qualification, then their human reality offers suitable, even excellent metaphor for speaking about divine mystery, who remains always ever greater.[4]

Women are not only the image of God but are also the image of Christ, a concept that is much harder to grasp. Women have been denied the right to serve their Lord in performing the sacraments, preaching, teaching, even administering the affairs of the church, because they are not men and Jesus was a man. If being a man were the most essential thing about Jesus then certainly women would be excluded from ministry. However, in the New Testament it is not Jesus' sex that

---

4.   Ibid., 71.

is important. What sets him apart as unique and powerful is his teachings and his actions.

When we study the New Testament we find that in order to be in the image of Christ all a person needs to do is to live life as Christ lived it. We represent Christ on earth in who we are and in what we do. Through the power of the Holy Spirit believers, male and female, become the body of Christ. We, women and men alike, become the image of Christ.

Even though little mention is made of women disciples, we know there were women in his audiences when Jesus was teaching, preaching and doing his works of wonder. As women study the New Testament and interpret it for themselves new light is being shed on the place of women in the early church, not because they are changing words of scripture, but because it is becoming apparent that the role of women was hidden or ignored by the church leaders who came later. Even though women are not named among the twelve disciples and their ministries are not reported to any great extent in the book of Acts, Luke includes women among the disciples.

> Meanwhile Saul, still breathing threats and murder against the disciples of the Lord, went to the high priest and asked him for letters to the synagogues at Damascus, so that if he found any who belonged to the Way, men or women, he might bring them bound to Jerusalem. (Acts 1:9)

Women were part of the group called the Way, the early followers of Jesus. Women must have been accepted as leaders in the early Christian movement because Paul is authorized to persecute the women as well as the men of the Way. The women, too, were a threat to the power of the synagogue and the state.

As the story unfolds, we are told that Saul saw a flash of light and fell to the ground. A voice asked, "Saul, Saul, why do you persecute me?" Saul then asked, "Who are you, Lord?" Jesus answered, "I am Jesus, whom you are persecuting." Saul had been party to killing the followers of Jesus, not Jesus himself who had already risen from the dead. Yet Jesus used the words "persecuting me." It is obvious that Jesus considered these men and women to be his body. Years later Paul, formerly known as Saul, wrote, "As many of you as were baptized into Christ have clothed yourselves with Christ" (Gal 3:27).

Paul, who came to be remembered as the greatest of the first Christian missionaries, wrote letters to the churches he founded; letters which have contributed greatly to building and maintaining a position of subordination for women. However, he also wrote great statements in which he describes the body of Christ as made up of all believers, regardless of sex, race or degree of freedom. In Galatians 3:28, an early Christian baptismal hymn, Paul states that within the body of Christ the classifications of people made by the world do not apply in the body of Christ. Through baptism the believer puts on Christ. She becomes one with Christ. Paul elaborates on this thought in II Corinthians 5:17: "So if anyone is in Christ, there is a new creation." These new creatures will now participate equally—as one flesh—in the life, death and resurrection of Christ. Whether our bodies are male or female we are one in Christ and equal in his eyes. What makes Jesus the Savior of us all is not that he was a man, but that the fullness of God dwells in him; that he suffers in solidarity with all those who suffer oppression and degradation; that he seeks to set all people free from whatever keeps them from having life abundant.

Paul gets the credit or the blame, depending on one's viewpoint, for making sexist statements that have kept women in a second place position ever since he wrote them, but his passages about the members of the community include women as surely as men.

> And all of us, with unveiled faces, seeing the glory of the Lord as though reflected in a mirror, are being transformed into the same image from one degree of glory to another; for this comes from the Lord, the Spirit. (II Cor 3:18)

> For those whom he knew he also predestined to be conformed to the image of his Son, in order that he might be the firstborn within a large family. (Rom 8:29)

Women share in the essence of Christian faith in the same degree that men do. When they understand and accept this equality, women are enabled to experience and to speak of themselves as valuable, active participants in history. In the light of the generations of negative feelings toward women and their abilities, this new feeling of power and worth is similar to conversion, an act of faith that is central to the Christian life.

Conversion may be defined as changing from one religion to another or from a sinful life to a life of righteousness. From a conservative Christian viewpoint conversion describes an event that only happens once, can be pinpointed by date and place of occurrence and is a turning from a life of sin to a life of righteousness. It is referred to as being born again. In liberal Christian thought it is believed that conversion happens over and over again, sometimes on a daily basis, since it is recognized that even with a deep commitment to God a person continues to sin, to do things that are opposite to the will and nature of God.

A classic definition of conversion is turning around and going a new direction. For example, a person who is living life apart from God may at some point feel the need for connection to God, to turn her life around and accept God into her life. This definition of conversion can be applied to what happens to women when they realize that they have been marginalized by patriarchy and begin to understand that they are *good, active participants* in history. Dr. Johnson uses three nouns to describe this action: contrast, confirmation, conversion. First comes a sense that the way things are is not right and must change: women are more valuable than society treats them. At this point a woman may choose either to close her eyes to the situation or act to change it. Next comes confirmation found in the value of their own lives, in the lives of friends and contemporary women, and in the long-silenced stories of women and movements that substantiate the value of women. Third is the conversion which says no to sexism and yes to the goodness of being women. They turn from devaluing themselves as they have been devalued and see the remarkable contributions to the flourishing of the world that women of the past have made, that women of the present are making and that women of the future will make.

Jesus called people to turn (conversion) and follow him, a decision that means giving up old roles and taking on new ones. Matthew, Mark and Luke all tell the story, each in his own way, of the discussion of the disciples about who was the greatest among them. According to all three, Jesus' answer to this debate was to draw a child up beside him to say, "Whoever welcomes this child in my name welcomes me, and whoever welcomes me welcomes the one who sent me; for the least among all of you is the greatest" (Lk 9:48). In Mark's Gospel Jesus says, "Whoever wants to be first must be last of all and servant of all" (Mk 9:35). To be converted, to be who Jesus wants us to be, we must turn from self-importance to self-giving, from conceit to humility, from putting ourselves first to putting ourselves last.

Unexpectedly, in the light of culture's dualistic view of gender, Jesus asks his followers to become more woman-like. He asks all of us, men and women, to take on the role of that half of the human population who, by gender definitions, are weaker and less important. If Jesus is God incarnate, as Christians believe, then the characteristics of God which he reveals are, by gender definition, feminine: compassion, humility, love of others, giving one's life for others. Adoption of these new roles is a big step for many men to take and may be why there are more women than men who are Christians.

The detrimental impact of this ideal for Christian behavior is that for women it adds to their tendency to self-depreciation which is already deeply imbedded in their psyches by the force of negative ideas about and the denigrating treatment of women. For women, as for slaves and other suppressed people, the embracing of this servant role as part of God's will and plan can be a way to legitimate their being kept in submission. The force used to keep them in their place has been the idea that what God desires of people is service and obedience therefore they must obey their masters whoever that may be and however they themselves are treated.

Conversion is not only a theological concept, it is also a real life experience which is attested to over and over again by people of all ages and times. However it needs to be re-interpreted in the light of women's experience. The emphasis on the need for a person to be converted from sin and selfishness to humility and servanthood is dangerous to the well being of women. Most women already see themselves as servants of others, and are treated as such. The conversion experience that most women need is to be converted from thinking of themselves as having been created inferior, using their station in life as an excuse for not pushing themselves to become the person God created them to be. Women are as sinful as men, but one sin for which they need forgiveness is that of accepting the role of a subordinate and thinking they can be nothing else.

In countless ways women are newly involved in experiencing and expressing themselves as active subjects of history and not just as objects. Because of the negative assessment of women's humanity under patriarchy, these acts of women seeing their worth and speaking it can be described in Dr. Johnson's words as

> ...a turning away from trivialization and deformation of oneself as a female person and turning toward oneself as worthwhile, as in fact a gift, in community with others similarly changing. This conversion amounts to nothing less than a rebirth....[5]

The conversion that women need is not an experience of denying oneself, but of accepting the empowerment of oneself. For a woman this conversion can be described as a rebirth just as the traditional conversion process is described. By realizing her own value in God's eyes, she is reborn. The conversion process as we have understood it is a coming face to face with what is wrong in oneself, seeing it as something that needs to be remedied. When women come face to face with themselves and see that they are buying into a system which says they are inferior,

---

5.   Ibid., 62.

they can change their attitudes about themselves and about other women so that they affirm the value of the feminine.

When women accept the reality that their value has been denied or limited, not by the way they have been created by God but by a patriarchal society, they can begin to speak about their own goodness and value, about their own power in playing an active role in history. Accepting the power of their own reality happens when women remember and tell their own stories, the stories of the women in their lives, and the stories of women from the past who did strong things not expected from a woman. Joan of Arc, Madame Curie and Florence Nightingale were held up for me as women who did great things but they were lauded for being the exception among women. There have been heroic, smart, active women in all ages in all places but that reality has been systematically overlooked.

As the discipline of women's studies has taken shape and gained importance, we are learning more and more about the hidden side of the history of our country and of the world: the history made by women. From the novels, autobiographies, letters and diaries written by women it is possible to recover the role which women have played on the stage of world history. A good example of this search for the real story about women's roles is found in the book, *The Women's West,* edited by Susan Armitage and Elizabeth Jameson. The essays in this book are about the variety of ways women of all ethnic groups were involved in the history of the western part of the United States. In contrast to Hollywood's version of the West which contained only two types of women—the good wife and the bad harlot—many types of women and the roles they played are being discovered as attention is paid to the stories told about themselves by the women of the West. We are encouraged and strengthened when we read of women past and present. Then we realize that women were indeed present making history even though their contributions to society have been largely ignored and undervalued. History is not made by men alone, but by women and men working together.

Women need to share their very own stories with each other. When the gender roles are accepted without question, women hesitate to talk with each other about what is happening to them because it may seem there is something wrong with them or with their most important relationships, or else they don't want to place the men in their lives in a bad light. Only when they share their stories do they realize that other women also hide things about themselves and their lives. Further this secrecy is detrimental to themselves, their children, and their husbands since it prevents women from being fully who they are and robs the others in their lives of the ability to understand and appreciate them.

When people say "no" to the past treatment of women and "yes" to the strength, intelligence, creativity and goodness of women conversion happens. Conversion happens when women who have been taken for granted, women who have been treated as inferior, women who have kept their light under a bushel for fear of seeming unfeminine speak up for themselves and show their gifts proudly. Conversion brings hope for a future that will be better for women, men, and children allowing the value of all people to be appreciated.

When we use the concept of conversion to take a serious look at women's experience of finding their value we experience God in new ways.

> …women's awakening to their own human worth can be interpreted at the same time as a new experience of God, so that what is arguably occurring is a new event in the religious history of humankind.[6]

With this new event comes a new understanding of the value of women's bodies, the value of their need for connectedness, the value of "feminine" characteristics such as nurturing and caring for others which show that female as well as male is created in the image of God. Now "what is fitting for the mystery of God to be and to do receives new contours."[7] Now we can speak of God in feminine terms because who women are as human beings has been accepted and comes to be valued. Since women are created in the image of God just as men are, their human experience can also be used in making metaphors as we learn to speak about the Divine Mystery. It is not an "insult" to God to be called by any feminine metaphor or to be referred to with feminine pronouns.

---

6. Ibid., 62.
7. Ibid., 62.

5

Scripture

The grass withers, the flower fades; but the word of our God will stand forever. (Isaiah 40:8)

Your word is a lamp to my feet and a light to my path. (Psalms 119:105)

The search for emancipatory speech about God leads through the path of women's historical experience to the Bible, the literary precipitate of the founding religious experiences of the Jewish and Christian communities and a continuing resource for their life. [1]

"Jesus loves me! This I know, for the Bible tells me so." Singing this children's song is my first memory of Sunday school and church. Sitting on a chair that was so high my feet didn't touch the floor, I knew that Jesus loved me not because the Bible told me so—I couldn't read—but because my Sunday School teachers who could read the Bible loved me. An integral part of the foundation for my future spiritual life was laid by those women who showed me, a little child, what they knew to be true in the Bible. The way those faithful women treated me and the other children taught me that Jesus loves me.

The 1940s, when I was in elementary school, were years when memorizing Bible verses was an important part of each Sunday school lesson. I did diligently and joyfully memorize all the Scripture passages that were assigned to me and

---

1.   Ibid., 76

proudly won a book of missionary stories for memorizing ten passages and reciting them perfectly to the teacher.

However, as I recall these times, I don't remember being taught any stories about little girls. There were little boys: Samuel, David, Jesus. Except for Mary the mother of Jesus, the best stories were about men and boys. I do remember Sarah and Rachel for being mothers of important sons; and of course Lot's wife whose claim to fame was that she disobeyed God and got the punishment she deserved, being turned into a pillar of salt. I certainly didn't want to be in that one! The stories were about women in relation to their fathers, their husbands and their sons, but few of them had value in and of themselves. Still I knew that Jesus loved me.

During our junior high years one of my younger sisters and I took turns choosing Bible passages to memorize and recite to each other. The passages we chose were never stories, but were passages that spoke to us about the kind of persons we should be. The Beatitudes were our favorite because in these precious words we saw how we wanted to live our lives. We learned passages that taught us how to be and how to act as children of God, even though so much of what we studied was addressed to men. By the wisdom and grace of God we were enabled to hear words addressed by men to men as words which could also inspire young girls in their search for relationship with God.

Remembering those years now, I know that what helped me grow in my relationship with God was not the Bible, even as much as I loved it, but rather it was Jesus Christ by the power of the Holy Spirit at work in my heart. Some feminists have given up on the Bible entirely saying it is so male oriented that it can be of no use to women. It can't be fixed. However, based on my own experience, I believe the Bible is one of the most important ways that God speaks to her people and is not beyond hope. Now that there are women scholars at work in the fields of Biblical and other ancient languages, archeology, ancient history, classical theology, philosophy and other fields of research that touch on aspects of the Bible, women and men scholars are discovering ways to understand the Bible that recognize the God given value of women. But, even more importantly, the fact that millions of women through the ages have loved and served the Christian God portrayed in the Bible says that it is not the Bible itself that touches hearts, but rather the Spirit of God who loves the hearts of people into faith as they read and cherish the Scriptures.

Bible study during my college years was centered around English major classes that focused on great literature including the Bible. Even from that viewpoint the Spirit worked in me to make the patriarchal words of Scripture a vital part of my spiritual life. There is no doubt in my mind but that the Holy Spirit called me into the ministry using not only the influence of the Bible but also of those who had taught me from it through all my growing up years.

In seminary studying the Greek and Hebrew texts was such a new and enlivening way of reading the Bible that I saw many things in the Scriptures I had never seen before. Until then the Bible had been interpreted for me, not by me. With the tools, such as the original languages, the historical context, and the history of the early church, to unlock meanings not touched by my teachers before, I began to see the depth of meaning of the words and the possibilities for differing interpretations of the meaning of various passages. Still, I did not consciously recognize that these experiences of God were always from a male point of view. What was important to me then was that I learned that ideas and stories in the Bible could be told and interpreted in different ways. I can see now that during all my years of study of the Bible I had seen it as speaking to males directly and to me indirectly. To a certain extent I was reading the stories and then reinterpreting them so that I could find the meaning they had for me as a woman.

Even when I felt called by God to be a minister and my denomination would allow it, I saw myself as ill-suited to be a pastor of congregation as a man could be so I decided I would become a missionary. I had always loved Africa and thought that was where I would serve. It was not that I thought missionaries were a less important part of church work, but I knew that historically it was on the mission field where women were accepted as professionals even though they could not be ordained. The prevailing thought among clergy and laity alike in those early years of the ordination of women was that finding a minister for a husband must be the only reason a woman would want to go to seminary. And sure enough, when I appeared before my presbytery to be examined about my "call" the first question asked was, "Are you going to seminary just to find a minister for a husband?" This very question was such an affront to me because I had heard God call me in an almost audible voice to serve the church as a minister. Little did those men know that a timid woman like me would never, ever have chosen on her own to do such a bold thing as to seek ordination at any time let alone at a time when it was a pioneer role!

Most of my life I did not question the ideas and feelings about the second class position women had been assigned in the church and in society, even though I did protest that same kind of treatment of people of color and people in poverty. If someone had asked me about the truth and fairness of the exclusion of women and girls from importance in the life of faith, I am sure I would have defended it by saying, "That is the way God intends things to be."

However, not long after I started reading books by feminist theologians I became aware that the inferior position of women is not God's idea but has been dictated by a history of thought, including the story of salvation, which was written primarily by men. Women are not absent from history because they were solely occupied with serving husbands and bearing and raising sons, but because men were the teachers, writers and editors. These men decided, on the basis of their male experience what and who was important enough to be included. Writing on any topic reflects the viewpoint of the writer. Since the Bible was written by males it reflects the viewpoint of males. This is also true of the academic disciplines of science, philosophy, psychology, sociology, history and theology.

Even though there are some female and cosmic images of God in the Bible, male images predominate because in the understanding of the biblical authors, women were subordinate. Since these writers lived in a society that was completely patriarchal, God was called king, lord, father, ruler and master, or indirectly referred to with masculine pronouns.

While recognizing that the society in which the biblical writers lived placed women under the power of men in a hierarchical structure, people can and do still believe that the masculine names for God are God-given and cannot be changed or even questioned. Some believe that the revelation of God's will comes only in the form of truth given by God to human beings in verbal form and written down by them exclusively in the Bible. With this frame of reference the Bible stories and teachings have to be accepted as true exactly as they are told and cannot be questioned. Consequently, interpretation consists of simple literal repetition. The words and their meaning are written in stone. If this is the only way to view the word of God in the Bible then the church has no option but to continue to use only masculine metaphors for God, the metaphors of ruling men.

An example of taking the Bible literally are people today who spend their time trying to prove that the date scientists give for the existence of the dinosaurs is wrong. In their worldview the world has to have been created within the time frame which they have figured out based on their calculations of dates recorded in the Bible. People who read the Bible as literal truth also believe that if the whole Bible is not true word for word then none of it is true. However, the Bible wasn't written to teach the natural sciences nor to give chronological information about political history, but to witness to God's love, grace and action in the midst of a broken world.

Over time theology has found that other modes of revelation besides the Bible contribute to our attempts to know God. Historical events, inner experiences, logical discussions, and symbolic meditation are helpful and appropriate in the continuing human search for relationship with God. Each of these modes of interpretation has its own strengths and weaknesses, but because we are each different from another, we learn and understand in different ways. We need to interpret the Scriptures under the guidance of the Holy Spirit in our own unique way so that we are enabled to be in fellowship with God. The nature, value, and life of the Bible is not that it is written in stone, but that it is alive and fluid and speaks to different people in different ways in different times and different places.

Interpreting, explaining and passing on the meaning of Scripture is a continuing process done by groups of people living the faith together including congregations in worship and Bible study, people in conferences and retreats applying Scripture to denominational and private life, students and teachers in Christian seminaries. These people are communities of men and women bringing many different viewpoints to the table in work that could also be exploring feminine language for God in the struggle for emancipation from sexism and the horrors it causes.

"Horrors" seems like too strong a word for a middle-class white woman in the United States to use, but it describes what sexism does to women in nations all over the world. In the United States we talk about women being held down in their professions by the glass ceiling as being sexism, and it is. But sexism also contributes mightily to the hunger and starvation of women and girls in the United States and around the world; to the physical abuse of women in their own homes; to the danger for women in public places; to the oppression of women in societies considered less developed than ours; to the selling of girls and boys into sexual slavery; and to the female circumcision practiced widely in some societies. It is sexism that accounts for the fact that one out of three women in the world cannot read or write. Sexism underlies the fact that out of the one billion people in the world who live in poverty, 70%, are women. Education of women should be one of the most important items on the agenda of the world's nations because the advancement of women is essential to the well-being and progress of every society and of the global community. When women are educated birth rates decline, infant mortality decreases, and immunization rates rise. All three results combined mean a smaller, healthier world population which would lead to better uses of the world's natural resources while at the same time providing the food that is so desperately needed worldwide.

Women and men who are seeking to free people from fear and degradation of all kinds, including sexism, are guided by a liberating impulse that comes from the Bible. The healing, redeeming, liberating pattern of the story of the God of Israel, the God of Jesus, through the worst times of history provides a guide for reading the Bible. In applying that guide some texts fade in importance and others which have been neglected move to the forefront. An example of such a change is in the question of slavery which from ancient times was taken to be the will of God.

> After much anguish and debate in the nineteenth century, and with this implicit understanding, the slavery texts of the Bible were laid aside and no longer guide Christian discourse and behavior, for rather than contribute to the good news of salvation they long sustained a genuinely evil social institution. The same dynamic now directs the interpretation of sexist biblical texts that in an analogous way can be judged according to the norm of whether they release salvation for the most abused of women. It is most emphatically not salvific to diminish the image of God in women, to designate them as symbols of temptation and evil, to relegate them to the margins of significance, to suppress the memory of their suffering and creative power, and to legitimate their subordination.[2]

As liberating discussion based on the experience of women increases, biblical language about God in female metaphors becomes a rich revelation of new depths of faith.

Since the New Testament is the preeminent source for Christians for understanding faith, it is of the utmost importance that we consider the passages therein not only as we have always been taught, but also to realize that these words too were written mainly by men from the standpoint of men in a culture that favored men. We need to read Scripture in ways that will help us understand what part women actually played but which were not recorded. We need to find new ways to look at the relationship of the masculine and the feminine in our faith. For many people today, it is easy to reinterpret Old Testament passages because some of them are at odds with the scientific knowledge we have at our disposal It is much more difficult to see the words of the New Testament in a new light because as Christians it is the life blood of our spirits. If we are to free women, men, girls, boys and the creation from the global arrangement that keeps so many people living lives of desperate need, and at the same time destroys our environment, we need to take a look at the Gospels through a new lens.

The Fatherhood of God is arguably the most crucial concept of the New Testament for us to reexamine. Since Jesus called God "Father," the paternal metaphor is so normative for the church that other names for God are neglected or excluded from our worship and study. The prevailing argument insists that Jesus'

---

2.   Ibid., 79.

example and teaching make the metaphor of father the most appropriate one for the church to use, a position that results in the exclusion of feminine metaphors for God. The problem is that the predominant or sole use of the address "Father" singles out one particular motif from the many Jesus used when he was teaching and leaves out other names which Jesus used to describe God, names which are also filled with rich meaning. In effect, we are robbed of the variety of ways that Jesus named God.

The argument here is not against the use of the name "Father." It is against using the father metaphor to the exclusion of other scriptural metaphors which have the power to enrich not only our personal devotions, but our understanding of the nature of God's activity in the world. The exclusive use of the name, Father, is not the result of Jesus using it as his main or only name for God, but rather is a result of theological development in the early church after the death and resurrection of Jesus.

The theological development of the idea of God as Father can be seen as it grows in the Gospels. In these writings the number of times the word "father," referring to God, is used increases in relation to the date of the writing. The later the writing the more it is used. Mark, the earliest of the Gospels uses the word four times, Luke fifteen times and Matthew forty-nine times. The Gospel of John, last to be written uses the name "Father" one hundred and nine times. The study of the origins of the Gospels is fascinating, but is too involved to engage in here, suffice it to say that there were earlier, possibly unwritten, traditions from which the Gospel writers drew in telling the story of Jesus. These sources are called Mark, Q, special Luke, special Matthew and John. In these sources Mark uses the name Father for God once, Q once, special Luke twice, special Matthew once. The latest of them, John, refers to God as Father seventy-three times. These numbers illustrate that as time passed and patriarchal ideas and practices of the Roman world encroached on the church, the use of the name father for God increased. Christian thought was changing from the egalitarian ideas of Jesus into the patriarchal thought of the Roman society in which the church needed to survive.

"Abba" is the Aramaic word for father which is used by the Gospel writers. It actually means "Daddy." One of my very young friends was deserted by his father before he was born. When this child describes his father he says, "He is my father. He is not my Dad." This five year old child's wisdom directs us to the understanding not that God as Father deserts us or loves us less, but rather to show that "Dad" is a more intimate term. When Jesus called God Father, he meant it to show the intimacy of the relationship between himself and God. He meant it to show that God loved him as a Daddy would. It is not a dominating male figure whom Jesus calls Father. Rather, it is a Being who seeks intimacy, who has compassion in the face of suffering, who wills good in the midst of evil. The way Jesus taught about God is subversive of any form of domination or attempt to dominate and undermines any feeling or belief that anyone is less valuable to God than anyone else. The gift of salvation coming from God through Jesus in the Spirit turns power relationships upside down.

> The one gift of salvation coming from God through Jesus-Sophia in the Spirit upends power relationships, transforming all teachers, fathers, masters, great ones into servants of the little ones. By exalting the lowly and humbling the mighty it creates relationships that circle back and forth in the solidarity of sisters and brothers rather than up and down in graded ranks. Jesus' Abba signifies a compassionate, liberating God who is grossly distorted when made into a symbol and supporter of patriarchal rule.[3]

In the Bible there are symbols besides father and other masculine images for God that we can choose to enrich our understanding of God's being and activity and thereby deepen our own faith and spiritual life. Three symbols which we will consider in some detail are Spirit, Wisdom, and Mother. These feminine symbols are so entangled in a framework that is male dominated that they cannot be taken simply at face value. However, considered within a different framework that affirms the equal political, social and economic rights of all people, these metaphors have the power to liberate men, women and children.

Spirit is one of the words most commonly used when the Bible speaks about God's creative presence and activity in the world. The word "Spirit" shows us God who is alive and active in our midst. This is not God who is high and lifted up on a throne in heaven isolated from his subjects. Rather, it is God who creates, sustains and guides all things. This God who has a hand in all that happens cannot be confined to a given place, a given time or a given activity. John says the Spirit, like the wind, blows where it chooses and we don't know where it comes from or where it goes (Jn 3:8). Divine Spirit is not understood as a being separate from God but rather as the creating and freeing power of God in the world.

The Bible was written originally in Hebrew and Greek and was first translated into Latin. Each of these three languages has a word for spirit: the Hebrew *ruah,* which is grammatically feminine; Greek *pneuma,* which is grammatically neuter; Latin *spiritus,* which is grammatically masculine. Jerome, a Bible translator and

---

3.   Ibid., 82.

theologian in the late fourth century, taught that these three words signify that God is above all categories of sexuality and is indeed Spirit. While the gender implications of the words used for spirit are inconclusive as to whether we should call God he or she, the Biblical contexts in which they are found provide a legitimate key to the use of feminine as well as masculine names for God.

The imagery used of the Spirit and the works credited to the Spirit in Hebrew Scriptures give us clues that it is appropriate to speak about the Spirit in terms which reflect women's experience. *Ruah's* activities as recounted in the Bible include the very activities that have engaged generations of women: creating new life; working to nourish, sustain and protect that life in myriad ways; renewing and repairing that which has been damaged; grieving over harm and destruction; comforting others in their grief; teaching their own children and the children of others how to live in wholesome ways in this world. Some specific images taken from what has always been considered "women's work" are that of a woman knitting together a life in her womb (Ps 139:13); a woman in the pangs of childbirth (Is 42:14); a midwife (Ps 22:9-10); a mother's responsibility (Num 11:11-12); a washerwoman (Is 4:4).

Feminine metaphors for the Spirit are not limited to the Hebrew Scriptures. Christian Scriptures continue the tradition of speaking of the Spirit in connection with the ministry and resurrection of Jesus Christ and the growth of the community of the disciples. In the New Testament, Spirit shows the power of God at work in Jesus' teaching and healing. Everything Jesus did, he did by the power of the Spirit dwelling within him. Believers in Jesus as the Christ experience the life and presence of the risen Christ and the power of the new life in him through the work of the Spirit in their own lives.

Three metaphors used in the New Testament which convey the feminine nature of the Spirit are dove, birth, and paraclete. Luke wrote that when Jesus was baptized the Spirit descended upon him in the form of a dove, an image that has been meaningful through the ages and continues to be meaningful to Christians today as they try to "picture" the Holy Spirit. A surprising and somewhat unsettling fact about the dove is that:

> In Greek mythology, as Ann Belford Ulanov points out, the dove is the emblem of Aphrodite, the goddess of love. Doves were even cultically protected, with towers erected for them and a steady supply of food provided. The figure of the dove in Christian art thus links the Holy Spirit with the broad pre-Christian tradition of divine female power: "Iconographically, the dove is a messenger of the goddess and of the Holy Spirit."[4]

---

4.   Ibid., 84.

Rejecting it as heresy is most Christians' first reaction to this comparison, but in the search for inclusive names for God it provides a stepping stone on the way to seeing God's image as both male and female. The study of the history of ancient deities strongly suggests that the feminine has been a part of divinity from the most ancient of times.

The birth image is also strong in the New Testament. In the third chapter of John's Gospel, Jesus had a conversation with Nicodemus, a leading Pharisee. In response to Nicodemus' statement of belief in Jesus as a teacher who has come from God, Jesus said, "...no one can see the kingdom of God without being born from above" (John 3:3). Nicodemus took literally Jesus' words about being born again and asked how it is possible to return to his mother's womb and be born again. Jesus answered that what is born of the flesh is flesh and what is born of the Spirit is spirit. Jesus used a metaphor to explain to Nicodemus what needs to happen in his life if he is to become a follower. We have said before that using a metaphor is taking something we know and likening it to something we don't know in order to understand the unknown better. Jesus is telling us something about God (the unknown) when he says we must be born (the known) of the Spirit. Being born of the Spirit most surely conveys the idea of the femaleness of God since males do not give birth. God, like a mother, gives birth to us. To say "*he* gives birth to us" is patriarchal language that hides the aspect of God which includes the female. It would help us understand God more truly to stand with the facts of nature and affirm that God *the Mother* is the source of our birth and of our rebirth.

The word, "paraclete," along with the words "dove" and "birth," carries ideas of the feminine. In classical Greek, the noun, paraclete, is derived from the verb which means "to call to one's aid." Thus, as a noun, it conveys the idea of advocate or intercessor and is used four times in the Gospel of John (14:16, 26; 15:26; 16:7) in the setting of the Last Supper The disciples understood only vaguely, from what Jesus had been saying and from what was going on in the city outside their door, that something terrible was about to happen to their beloved Rabbi. They were about to be separated from their beloved friend and teacher. In order to comfort them Jesus said, "Do not let not your hearts be troubled, believe in God, believe also in me" (John 14:1). "I will not leave you orphaned; I am coming to you. In a little while the world will no longer see me, but you will see me; because I live, you also will live" (14:18,19). "I have said these things to you, while I am still with you. But the Advocate (in Greek the paraclete), the Holy Spirit, whom the Father will send in my name, will teach you everything, and remind you of all that I have said to you" (14:25-26). After Jesus' ascension, the work of the Spirit, the Paraclete, is to abide with the disciples, teaching, reminding, maintaining, and completing the work of Jesus.

When these three metaphors—dove, birth and paraclete—are brought together with the female roles that surround the Spirit a strong and useful language arises. Elizabeth Johnson quoted Jay Williams from an article in *Theology Today:*

> "In the divine economy it is not the feminine person who remains hidden and at home. She is God in the world, moving, stirring up, revealing, and interceding. It is she who calls out, sanctifies, and animates the church. Hers is the water of one baptism. The debt of sin is wiped away by her. She is the life-giver who raises men {sic} from the dead with the life of the coming age. Jesus himself left the earth so that she, the intercessor, might come."[5]

Another name for the Spirit of God is Shekinah which is a female symbol used extensively by early Jewish scholars. They worked diligently after the Hebrew biblical canon was closed to interpret and to understand what these writings meant and how they were to be applied to daily life. The Hebrew verb that is the root of the word, Shekinah, means "to dwell", and is used in Jewish writings as a synonym for God's presence among the people. In Exodus 25:8, God said to Moses that he should tell the people to make a sanctuary so that "I may dwell among them." This is Shekinah. This is She Who Dwells with the people. Shekinah says, "I will dwell among the Israelites and I will be their God. And they shall know that I am the Lord their God, who brought them out of the land of Egypt that I might dwell among them; I am the Lord their God" (Ex 29:45-46).

When we read Israel's history knowing the meaning of the word *Shekinah,* we see God's elusive, powerful being in the form of female presence. She showed herself in symbols of cloud, fire or radiant light that met the people, descended upon them, overshadowed them. Her most significant work was that of accompanying them or leading them so that wherever the righteous went, Shekinah went with them. She accompanied the Hebrew people through the wilderness and into and out of exile. Shekinah was with them giving them strength and reason to hope for a safe, settled future in a promised land. She was with them through the dark days and the golden days of the kingdom. She was with them as their beloved temple was desecrated and their holy city of Jerusalem burned. She accompanied them into exile in Babylon and after almost seventy years returned with them to their devastated city of Jerusalem to rebuild the temple and their

---

5.   Ibid., 85.

nation. Shekinah dwelt and still dwells with people through thick and through thin, through good times and through bad times. In good times she rejoices with the people and in bad times she suffers with them.

> Made familiar by long use throughout medieval kabbalistic writings, *shekinah,* is a term with female resonance that carries forward the biblical understanding of God's Spirit. It signifies no mere feminine dimension of God but God as She-Who-Dwells-Within, divine presence in compassionate engagement with the conflictual world, source of vitality and consolation in the struggle.[6]

Steeped in this tradition of Spirit and Shekinah it was only natural that Christians in the early centuries continued to use explicitly female imagery for God's Spirit. The early Christians in the Eastern (Syriac) tradition commonly used the image of the brooding or hovering mother bird to describe the activities of the Spirit. Other maternal actions ascribed to the Spirit were "mothering" Jesus into life at his conception in Mary's womb, empowering him into mission at his baptism and bringing believers to birth out of the watery womb of the baptismal font. An early prayer says, "The world considers you a merciful mother. Bring with you calm and peace, and spread your wings over our sinful times."[7] Over time this imagery of the feminine was taken by the male rulers of the church, and given to Mary the mother of Jesus and to the institution of the church called Holy Mother Church. The Church, the body of Christ is always referred to with feminine pronouns.

The most developed personification of God's presence and activity in the Hebrew Scriptures is Wisdom, another metaphor parallel to Spirit and Mother. The word itself is grammatically feminine: *hokmah* in Hebrew; *sophia* in Greek, *sapientia* in Latin. The fact that these words are feminine in gender does not by itself settle any argument about the nature of the Spirit; however, the Bible itself consistently depicts Wisdom as female. She is described as sister, mother, female beloved, cook, hostess and numerous other roles associated with women's work. These are the means by which Wisdom fills the world and interacts with nature and human beings to lure them along the path that leads to life.

Wisdom as a person, let alone a divine person, is a new and disturbing idea to most Christians because we take the word to mean knowledge or seasoned understanding, which is the clear meaning of the word when spoken of as an attribute to be sought after. But it is also quite clear that some passages about wisdom are

---

6.   Ibid., 86.
7.   Ibid., 86.

referring wisdom as a person not a quality. This wisdom is Holy Wisdom, Hagia Sophia, and is always feminine.

Proverbs 1, 8, 9 are the major wisdom poems found in the Old Testament which depict a personified figure who approaches human beings to call them into life. The descriptions of Sophia match descriptions of YHWH as he is portrayed in the Hebrew Scripture. She reflects the divine presence. In Proverbs, Wisdom/Sophia reveals herself as a street preacher who shouts her message condemning the evil activities of the people, promising punishment and redemption (1:20-33). She also shows herself as a bringer of peace (3:17); as creator (3:19); as the confidence of those who are afraid (3:24-26); as a giver of life (4:13); as a sister (7:4).

In Proverbs 8 she appears again as a street preacher in whose words are echoes of the prophetic promise of shalom—the promise of peace, justice and well-being for all people. In verse 22, Wisdom begins to show that she was with the Lord at creation, being the first of his acts of long ago. In verses 27-31, she confirms that she was there when he established the heavens; when he made the skies; when he assigned the limits of the sea; when he marked out the foundations of the earth. Furthermore, she was co-creator, rejoicing with him in the creation and delighting with him in the human race.

Sophia is described with similar passion and color in the Jewish Apocrypha in the books of The Wisdom of Solomon, Ecclesiasticus or The Wisdom of Jesus Son of Sirach, and Baruch which were included in the first translation of the Hebrew scriptures into Greek, the Septuagint. These books were rejected by the Jewish communities of Palestine and by rabbinic authorities of later times. The Apocrypha is printed between the testaments in many editions of the Bible today and is accepted as canonical by the Roman Catholic Church. Because Protestants do not accept it as canonical, it does not have the same authority in Protestant theology and is practically unknown to a large segment of Christianity. In contrast to the Jewish communities and rabbis who rejected them, they were accepted by the early Christian community as being appropriate for guiding its life and thought. They were part of the expression of the faith in the days of the early church. As first century Christians tried to express their experiences of salvation in Jesus Christ, they searched the Hebrew Scriptures and the Hellenistic culture for ways to proclaim the Good News in speech and in writing. In the process of that search they found frequently used names such as Son of God, Son of Man, Messiah and Logos, but they also found the names Wisdom/Sophia.

The Jewish tradition had already depicted Divine Sophia as having been sent by God to Jerusalem in the form of the Torah. Because the Jews believed that

God had sent Sophia to a particular place (Jerusalem) in a particular form (Torah) it was natural for the early Christians directly and indirectly to associate Jesus (a particular person) who was sent to Israel (a particular place) with Sophia. Her words, functions and characteristics quickly became associated with Jesus.

What Judaism said of Sophia, early Christian hymn writers and letter writers came to say of Jesus: he is the image of the invisible God, the firstborn of all creation (Col 1:15); the reflection of God's glory (Heb 1:3); the one through whom all things exist (I Cor 8:6); the one who calls out to those who are heavily burdened to come to him and find rest (Mt 11:28-30); the one who made people friends of God (Jn 15:15); and the one who gives eternal life to those who love him (Jn17:2). The same aspects of birthing, loving, caring, light-giving that describe Sophia fit Jesus as well.

> As the trajectory of wisdom Christology shows, Jesus was so closely associated with Sophia that by the end of the first century he is presented not only as a wisdom teacher, not only as a child and envoy of Sophia, but ultimately even as an embodiment of Sophia herself.[8]

The Gospel of Matthew, whose intended readers were Christians of both Jewish and Gentile origin, depicts Jesus as Sophia's child, showing her gracious goodness by befriending the outcast, delivering a prophetic message and preaching her ways even though such talk results in severe criticism. In Matthew 23:37-39, Jesus is described as a caring mother hen who, like Sophia, withdraws from a city that rejects him. Her brood under her wings, but being rejected by them. After the manner of Sophia he calls to all who are weary to come to him to find rest (11:28). Matthew not only uses Sophia's speech and deeds as he writes about Christ, but he also testifies to Sophia's intimate relationship with the one who is God of all by using words that previously had only been used of Sophia.

> At that time Jesus said, 'I thank you, Father, Lord of heaven and earth, because you have hidden these things from the wise and intelligent and revealed them to infants; yes, Father, for such was your gracious will. *All things have been handed over to me by my Father and no one knows the Son except the Father, and no one knows the Father except the Son and anyone to whom the Son chooses to reveal him.* (Mt 11:25-27) (Italics are mine.)

---

8.   Ibid., 95.

Elizabeth Johnson writes that the exclusivity of mutual knowledge expressed in this text from Matthew is biblically acknowledged elsewhere only of Sophia: only God knows Wisdom, and only Wisdom knows God. Accepting as authoritative the writings of the apocrypha, she cites passages from Baruch and from The Wisdom of Solomon to support this opinion, but it is also supported, as we have seen, by passages from the canon that Protestants accept such as Job 28:12-27 and Proverbs 1, 8, and 9.

The Gospel of John differs from the Synoptic Gospels not only because Matthew, Mark and Luke contain common material that is not found in John, but also because John makes frequent use of wisdom categories as he paints his portrait of Jesus. The prologue to the Gospel of John (1:1-18) influences the development of thought about Christ more than any other text from scripture. The "prehistory" of Jesus as John describes it is an echo of the story of Sophia which is found in Proverbs 8:22-31. According to John, the Logos, like Sophia, was present in the beginning, active in creating the world. He came from heaven to dwell among people and was rejected by some but gave light to others. Jesus/Wisdom is a radiant light that darkness cannot overcome. John's whole Gospel is punctuated with wisdom themes.[9]

The question becomes why did John use the title Logos instead of Sophia when, as we have seen, the works of Jesus/Logos reflect the works of Sophia so closely? One answer is: the apocryphal book, Wisdom of Solomon, had already directly equated *Logos* and *Sophia* in the act of creation.

> O God of my ancestors and Lord of mercy,
> who have made all things by your word (logos),
> and by your wisdom (sophia) have formed humankind...(Wisdom of Solomon 9:1-2)

As early writers and teachers worked to make the good news of Jesus Christ known to people it would have been appropriate and helpful in the light of traditional thought to use the word *sophia* instead of *logos*. John chose the word *logos* over the word *sophia* for at least three compelling reasons. The first is that although the early church knew Sophia well and prayed to her, there were still many goddess cults in existence at the time, and there was concern that worshipping Sophia would be mistakenly associated with these cults. It was vitally important for the early church to distinguish itself from other groups in order to avoid being assimilated into them and being identified with them.

---

9.   For example: John 1:1-18; 6:51, 7:28, 34, 37; 10:10, 14; 11:25; 14:6, 23; 15:15.

The second reason that the name *Logos* supplanted the name *Sophia* was that there was a group called Gnostics who did use the name of Sophia for Jesus. Eventually they were declared heretical, not because of their devotion to Sophia, but because they believed that Jesus was completely and only divine, that he had never really been a flesh and blood human being. In that setting to use the name Sophia and continue the connection between her and Jesus would have detracted from the firm belief that Jesus was fully human as well as fully divine. Thus, as the early church distanced itself from Gnosticism it also turned away from devotion to Sophia for fear of seeming to approve Gnostic beliefs.

The third reason the name *Sophia* was not used is because of the teachings of Philo, a Hellenistic Jewish philosopher who lived shortly after the birth of Christ. He had a major impact on first century theology. His work on the relationship of *sophia* to *logo* is complicated but it ends with *sophia* being disparaged because of her female character. Philo thought the female signified whatever is evil, whatever is tied to the world of senses, whatever is irrational and passive. At the same time he equated maleness with good, with the world of the spirit, rationality and active initiative. Dr Johnson quotes these words from Philo:

> For pre-eminence always pertains to the masculine, and the feminine always comes short of it and is lesser than it. Let us, then pay no heed to the discrepancy in the gender of the words, and say that the daughter of God, even Sophia, is not only masculine but father, sowing and begetting in souls aptness to learn, discipline, knowledge, sound sense, and laudable actions.[10]

Philo co-opts Sophia, a feminine figure: "makes" her masculine, "makes" her father, to the effect that even her life-bearing nature is translated into seed-sowing manliness. This is contrary to the whole history of Sophia imagery. Philo applies the tools of patriarchy to accomplish Sophia's elimination. Recalling that Philo was Jewish helps us to understand how pervasive this attitude and its effect were at that time. Concepts which prevailed in that Roman society took root across the western world, stimulating and cementing gender dualism.

Some would say substituting the masculine for *Sophia* was unavoidable because Jesus was a man and therefore the word *logos* fits Jesus better because of his sex. But in the sixty or so years before the Gospel of John was written it had been easy for believers to associate Jesus Christ with the feminine Sophia. The association was easy to make not only with the risen and exalted Christ, but even with the historical Jesus and his earthly ministry. Unfortunately for women and

---

10.   Johnson, *She Who Is,* Ibid., 98.

for the church, at the same time there was a big shift happening in the churches which was expressed in more hierarchical forms of governing and leading which excluded women from ministries in which they had been involved during Jesus ministry and immediately after his ascension. As sexism grew in the church, Sophia was suppressed.

The use of Wisdom categories in the early days of the church had profound theological consequences. The theology of Sophia/Wisdom enabled believers to see the crucified Jesus as having cosmic significance, relating him to the creation and governance of the world. It was also the vehicle used to describe Jesus as divine, as wholly God. None of the other Hebrew scriptural terms that were used—Son of Man, Messiah, Son of God—connote divinity. Neither does the word logos, which is barely used in the Hebrew Scriptures.

Coming from a background and understanding of Sophia as a divine person made it easier for the early Christians to see the Christ in feminine form. This idea of Jesus as being Sophia seems heretical to us because we put all the emphasis on Jesus Christ being male and because we view Sophia as some kind of pagan goddess. Since we are discovering that early on in the history of the church, Jesus was depicted as divine Sophia, it is not unthinkable nor unbiblical for us to confess him as the incarnation of God imaged in female symbols. Accepting Wisdom theology we can say that Jesus is the human being Sophia became. Sophia and all that she does were fully present in Jesus in his teaching, preaching and healing.

The fluidity with which the earliest Christians viewed Jesus' gender breaks the stranglehold that masculine only usage has had on the thinking of Christians through the generations. We have said over and over that God is mystery and cannot be understood completely. Wisdom theology is not heretical but is a reflection of the deep mystery of God and opens a pathway to Christology that uses female symbols as well as male symbols and thus is an inclusive Christology.

Many times in the postbiblical period Sophia and Logos have been seen as coequal expressions of the one saving power and presence of God. Jesus Christ is the human being Sophia became. The wisdom imagery continued to be used but was passed on to Mary the mother of Jesus. The figure of Sophia was forgotten in liturgy and teaching but remained "in the biblical text as a startling female personification of the mystery of God in powerful and close engagement with the world."[11]

God is Mother as well as Shekinah and Sophia. We have seen that female imagery encompasses more than motherhood, but motherhood is still a powerful and appropriate metaphor to use in naming toward God. There is a whole con-

---

11. Ibid., 100.

stellation of biblical symbols for God that revolve around women's experience of bearing, birthing and rearing. Texts are widely scattered throughout the Bible that refer to God as conceiving, being pregnant, going into labor, delivering, midwifing, nursing, carrying, rearing.[12] The love, care and compassion expressed by these passages and others describe men as well as women; but it is the woman's love of the child in her womb that is the model for the metaphor of God as Mother.

When we talk about the holy mystery in the symbols of Spirit, Sophia and Mother we are providing glimpses of an alternative to historically dominant patriarchal language about God. That alternative allows all people, and society as a whole, the freedom to recognize themselves as valuable and equal in the sight of God. It frees them to see their world in a new way, apart from the old hierarchy which exalted some persons at the expense of others, valuing men, women and even children according to an imposed system of worth. These metaphors, long suppressed because they are feminine, enable all of us to view the world through the eyes of a mother who loves all her children without any favoritism, without any condemnation.

---

12.   Among these passages are Num. 11:12-13; Deut. 32:18; Ps. 22:1, 9-10; Is. 42:14, 63:13, 49:15.

6

Classical Theology

o o o o o o o o o o o o o o o o o o o o o o o o o o o o o o o o o o o

Since you saw no form when the LORD spoke to you at Horeb out of the fire, take care and watch yourselves closely, so that you do not act corruptly by making an idol for yourselves, in the form of any figure—the likeness of male or female, the likeness of any animal that is on the earth, the likeness of any winged bird that flies in the air, the likeness of anything that creeps on the ground, the likeness of any fish that is in the water under the earth. And when you look up to the heavens and see the sun, the moon, and the stars, all the host of heaven, do not be led astray and bow down to them and serve them, things that the LORD your God has allotted to all the peoples everywhere under heaven. (Deuteronomy 4:15-19)

In essence, God's unlikeness to the corporal and spiritual finite world is total. Hence human beings simply cannot understand God. No human concept, word, or image, all of which originate in experience of created reality, can circum-scribe divine reality, nor can any human construct express with any measure of adequacy the mystery of God who is ineffable. [1]

The scene of the Hebrews worshipping the gigantic golden calf is one that I remember from my childhood Sunday school papers. The calf was so big and

---

1.　Johnson, *She Who Is,* 105.

gleaming golden and the people were dancing around gazing at it in awe and adoration. Even as a child I was amazed that these people whom God had so recently saved from the misery of slavery could so quickly turn to making and adoring a graven image. They had to know that God who heard their cries of anguish and saw their affliction was not this inanimate object created by their own hands. The God who freed them from slavery in Egypt was a God who felt love and compassion. The God who led them in the desert in the form of a cloud by day and a pillar of fire by night was a God who lived with them in their midst. On a daily basis they experienced this God as one who lived and moved and acted in their life, yet they turned to worship an idol in the shape of a calf who could neither speak nor move.

After receiving the Ten Commandments, the Hebrews in the desert and in all the generations to come obeyed with a passion the commandment not to make graven images of YHWH out of wood or metal or any other material. But what they did do was to portray him with words. They named him using a variety of word pictures. Sallie McFague writes:

> The strong iconoclasm of the Old Testament, its fear of making graven images of God, resulted in a superabundance of images, none of which was regarded as literal or even adequate.... The Hebrew poet piled up and threw away metaphors of God, in the hope of both overwhelming the imagination with the richness and undercutting any idolatrous inclination to absolutize images.[2]

In the generations since, human beings have narrowed that profusion of word images down to only male images, creating an idol of God, not literally a graven image, but nonetheless an idol. The fact that the exclusive use of male imagery for God cannot be questioned without accusations of heresy and/or paganism confirms that we have confined God basically to one shape, the male shape. We have created an idol of God. The great number and variety of images used in both the Hebrew Scriptures and the New Testament should remind us with every reading that God can and must be described in many ways. Our own personal experiences of God in worship and devotion, and in life and activity, bear witness to the fact that God is and does much, much more than a being described simply in masculine terms. However, we have a hard time thinking or speaking that truth. We have made an idol of maleness and called him God.

There is no short or simple answer to why this has happened. One aspect of the answer is that when anyone in any age thinks, writes, or talks about who God

---

2.   Sallie McFague, *Metaphorical Theology, Models of God in Religious Language* (Philadelphia: Fortress, 1982),42.

is and how to name God they must inevitably start from where they see God in their life. Since women have for the most part been shut out of avenues of making public their thoughts and experiences of God, we have a God and accompanying doctrines and creeds which have been debated and accepted by men. God is more than any human mind or gathering of minds together can comprehend. We are not privileged to know the mind or heart of God as though we were inside God's being. The only way we can name God is from our own experience—how we in our own lives and times have experienced God at work.

Throughout its history the Christian church has accumulated rich insights about the possibilities and the limitations of human thought and speech about God. The Gospels, the letters to the first Christian congregations, and the theology of the church fathers in the early centuries set forth a rich understanding of the nature of God, of God active in the lives of human beings. The theological thought of the early church teachers and preachers became codified in the theological works of medieval scholars, such as Thomas Aquinas, and is referred to as classical theology. There are at least three insights from classical theology which can guide us as we explore the possibilities of speaking about the mystery of God in ways that bring freedom to people who heretofore have been subordinated. The first insight is that God is incomprehensible. The second is that because God is incomprehensible we human beings can only speak about God using metaphors. The third is that since no one metaphor, no one name can define God we need to use many names for God.

God is incomprehensible. God remains a mystery not because she doesn't want humans to know her, nor because humans are too sinful for such knowledge, nor because some humans today are skeptical about religious matters. Rather, transcending all similarity to creatures and thus never to be fully known. is the nature of God. God is more than even the best, keenest, most spiritual human minds can comprehend. If God could be understood fully then God's "godness" would disappear.

Judaism and Christianity have always taught that even in revelation God remains wholly other, not revealing all there is to know about Godself, always present but beyond describing or explaining and so remaining God. This great mystery of God is expressed in Scriptures that tell us: God is unfathomable in the name God gives to Moses (Ex 3:14); no one sees God's form even in the making of the covenant (Deut 4:12, 15-16); God is God and not human (Num 23:19; Hos 11:9); God is beyond knowing (Job 36:26ff); God is a hidden God and impossible to compare with anyone or anything else (Isa 40:18, 25; 45:15).

The uniqueness of the Christian faith among world religions is the belief that God became a human being in Jesus of Nazareth in order to reveal Godself to the world. But even with such a real, live illustration of who God is and what God does, we still do not have the full revelation, the total picture of God's nature. New Testament passages remind believers that even after the advent of the Incarnate One, God is still incomprehensible. God cannot be captured in silver, gold, stone or any image formed by the art and imagination of humans (Acts 17:29). God dwells in unapproachable light, whom no human being has ever seen or can see (I Tim 6:16; Jn 1:18). The depth of God's wisdom and knowledge are unsearchable and no one has ever known the mind of God (Rom 11:33-36). God is even greater than our hearts and knows everything (I Jn 3:20). Even in Christ our knowledge is imperfect (I Cor 13:9, 12).

In the early centuries of Christianity biblical tradition and the Greek philosophical tradition found common ground in the idea that the human mind cannot comprehend the mystery of God's being nor can the human mind find an adequate name for God. The Greek philosophical tradition taught that God could not be named because the one ultimate origin of all things must be totally different from anything that human beings know. This idea was appealing to the early Christian theologians who were looking for ways to understand the scriptural theme that God while present in the world, is incomprehensible.

The ecumenical councils of the first centuries formulated dogma about the Trinity and about Christ that was intended to protect the mystery of divine greatness which they knew acted compassionately for the world's salvation. The very act of scholars gathered together for the purpose of debating and thinking through ideas about the nature of God made it dangerously easy to overlook the fact that they believed that God is by nature incomprehensible. The result of their debates had two opposite effects. On the one hand it protected God from all kinds of current and far-fetched ideas about who God is, and on the other hand it made God too small. It is a perilous but vital business to attempt to define God in terms of transcendence and mystery while at the same time recognizing that this One who is beyond human comprehension, having taken on human flesh and blood, also dwells among humans.

Augustine, one of the outstanding theologians in the history of the church,[3] expressed the consciousness of God's incomprehensibility by insisting that all

---

3.   Born in North Africa in 354 C.E. and died there in 450 C.E. He went through several stages of morality and theology, eventually becoming the Bishop of Hippo in North Africa. His writings include confessions, letters and sermons.

speaking about God comes from silence and ignorance and must return to silence and ignorance since God is too awesome to be named. He said:

> If you have understood, then this is not God. If you were able to understand, then you understood something else instead of God. If you were able to understand even partially, then you have deceived yourself with your own thoughts.[4]

He was not saying that we should give up on the work of knowing God but rather that we know God through loving for God is love.

> In loving, we already possess God as known better than we do the fellow human being whom we love. Much better, in fact, because God is nearer, more present, more certain.[5]

The love of God shown forth in the life of Jesus the Christ is the expression of God's presence with us in the midst of God's transcendence. Finding or creating a language to speak about God transcendent and God immanent is the work of believers of all generations in the struggle to name God.

The theological tradition of the early church fathers began to be incorporated into official teaching when the Fourth Lateran Council met in Rome in 1215. This council, which was caught up in a controversy over the Trinity, taught that the meaning of words differs when they are applied both to God and creatures. For instance, when the word "one" is applied to the disciples as being "one in us as we also are one" (Jn 17:22) it signifies a union of charity in grace. But when it is applied to the divine persons it means a unity of identity in nature. Another example is Jesus' words in Matthew 5:48: "you must be perfect as your heavenly Father is perfect." The word "perfect" means something different when applied to God than when applied to creatures. The understanding of the men at the Fourth Lateran Council is summed up in an important axiom: between Creator and creature no similarity can be expressed without implying that the dissimilarity between them is even greater. Hence, even though we are made in God's image God is always greater. God is always incomprehensible.

The second insight from classical theology is that we must use analogies to speak of God. In thinking about God we must start where we are. We can only use what we know as we attempt to explain the unexplainable. We cannot know

---

4.   Johnson, *She Who Is,* 108.
5.   Ibid., 108.

God from the inside of God, just as we can never know another person from the inside of that person. When we speak about or describe another person we are expressing what we have experienced of her through her actions and speech. When we dare to speak about God, the best words we can use come from our own experience of God's action and speech. As we experience the absolute mystery of God present and active in our individual lives and in the world, we can use the very best of human relationships and human qualities to point toward names for God.

As we speak to God, it is tempting to value the name we use as though it is somehow the one and only name for God. In order to avoid this pitfall medieval theologians said that speaking about God involves a threefold motion of affirmation, negation, and eminence. A word whose meaning is valued from human experience is used as a name for God (affirmation). Then the same word is denied as describing God because God is neither a human being nor a created object (negation). The third part of the motion is that God is more excellent than this word can ever describe (eminence). This third part does not deny the truth of the first part, but rather it says that the human limits of the word do not apply to God. It produces an awe and reverence that is dimmed when we use a single name for God and claim that name covers all there is to know about God.

For instance, God is a father (affirmation); God is not a father (negation); God is more than a father (eminence). If we go through this process with every word we use to describe our human experience with God there will open before us myriads of ways to name God, all of which will affirm God's presence in our lives while at the same time proclaiming that God is more than we can ever think or say.

When we understand that all language about God is metaphorical, we will become critical of any language used of God that declares itself the final and full understanding. The declaration that masculine images are the only legitimate way to speak about God must be contested because, if it isn't and then continues to be accepted as the only way to address God, it limits our sense of God's greatness and mystery. If there is to be an end to systems that restrict the rights, freedoms and well-being of any part of God's good creation, we must embrace new language about God.

Brian Wren, contemporary poet-theologian and hymn writer, says it clearly and gently:

> We shall only move beyond patriarchal idols if we name God with a variety of personal terms from human relationships, both female and male. At this stage

in our relationship to God, naming God in female terms is a priority, because it tilts our world from its patriarchal axis and enables us to meet the living God anew.[6]

The experience of females is just as valuable for naming God as is the experience of males. The negating aspects of analogy must be applied to the masculine metaphors for God. Calling God "he" is open to the same negation that all other analogies contain. God *is* he...God *is not* he...God *is more than he.* When women and men step back from calling God by masculine names exclusively, they are acknowledging the holy mystery of God. For women a refusal to call God only "he" is an affirmation of their own intrinsic worth. However, it must also be said that restricting words for God to only the feminine would be as inadequate and damaging as is restricting words for God to only the masculine.

The third insight is that, after we have admitted that God is incomprehensible and that we can only speak of God in analogies, then we must say again, as did classical theology, that *no one name ever defines God.* No single name ever says all there is to say about God. Even as we try to name God, God remains essentially incomprehensible. If we could name God with one all-encompassing name, we would have grasped the very essence of God, which our finite minds cannot do. Each name adds its own unique significance to our understanding of God and each name leans on the others to bring understanding.

The Bible and Christian tradition, as well as other religions and their holy writings, give evidence of an abundance of metaphors for the divine that feed our minds, expand our spirits, and strengthen our passion for justice for all. One of the real joys of studying how to name toward God is the discovery that there are a boundless number of names which can be used to call upon God and to describe God without violating God's sacredness. Some of these are terms taken from personal experience such as mother, father, husband, aunt, companion and friend as well as terms taken from political life such as advocate, liberator, king, and judge.

The Bible itself uses human professions to refer to God in action: dairymaid, shepherd, farmer, laundress, construction worker, potter, fisherman, midwife, merchant, physician, bakerwoman, teacher, writer, artist, nurse, metal worker, and homemaker. Even with the predominance of language from male experience there are places in the Bible where the activity of God is expressed in purely female terms: a woman giving birth, nursing her young, and caring for the little

---

6.   Brian Wren, *What Language Shall I Borrow? God-Talk in Worship: A Male Response to Feminine Theology* (New York: Crossroad, 1995), 161.

ones. Analogies from the animal world are also a source of names: a roaring lion, hovering mother bird, angry mother bear, and protective mother hen. In addition, the cosmos itself serves as a way to understand God: light, cloud, rock, fire, refreshing water, and life itself.

In his book, *One River, Many Wells,* Matthew Fox reports that other faiths also use many names for God. In the Hindu tradition it is said that there is only one God and he has a thousand names. In the Muslim tradition the practitioner recites and meditates on ninety-nine of the most beautiful names for God. Among those names are: The Provider, The Forgiver, the Most Great, The Truth, The Glorious, The Generous One. Thomas Aquinas, the Christian medieval theologian, offers a litany of names for God, all of which are taken from the Scripture: the Cause of All Things, the Beloved, the Eternal, the Knower, the Virtue.

Reading these lists and meditating on them has shown and continues to show me the magnificence of God in ways I have never thought or felt before. It seems as though I have been deprived of great possibilities for spiritual growth by the scarcity of names for God in my past spiritual life. The contrast is like a gray world and a world full of rainbow colors.

Besides enriching our spiritual lives, using more varied names for God can move us into actions that are ultimately more liberating for all creatures, human beings and the earth itself. Using a great variety of names for God opens up the beauty and value of all creation in the eyes of God and calls us to respect and protect it all. Even after we have prayed about, meditated on and used many names for God, we return to the silence which admits that God is still and always will be a Divine Mystery, a Being beyond our comprehension.

7

Spirit-Sophia

○ ○

*In the beginning when God created the heavens and the earth,
the earth was a formless void and darkness covered the face of
the deep, while a wind from God swept over the face of the
waters. (Genesis 1:1-2)*

*To refer to God's ongoing transcending engagement with the
world, theology, following one option among the several used
in Scripture, traditionally uses the word Spirit: the Spirit,
Holy Spirit, Spirit of God and, much less frequently, Spirit of
Christ. The term signifies a power that does not arise from
human initiative but undergirds and surrounds it in a relation that makes all else possible: the Creator Spirit at the very
heart of the world.* [1]

The life span of a violet under my care has been very short, but Grandma's violets
lived on and on. In the course of their lives they went through various stages of
growth under her love and care. The same has been true of God's love and care
for me. In the bleak days after Nancy, our eight-year old daughter, was found to
have juvenile diabetes, I felt God had let me down. I had spent the summer
before this diagnosis memorizing New Testament passages that promise you will
get what you ask for when you pray. On the way to the hospital I prayed that her
illness not be diabetes, but as soon as a nurse started an IV Nancy regained a
healthy, rosy color in her face and I knew the diagnosis was correct. Then I

---

1.   Johnson, *She Who Is,* 131.

prayed for Nancy to be healed, as I had for years prayed that our son, Jim, would be healed from asthma.

Countless numbers of people have stories of hitting rock bottom in various ways before things begin to change for the better in their lives and that is what happened to me in this period of my spiritual journey. Since Jim was a year and a half old, I had been praying fervently that God would heal him from the allergies that caused his severe asthma. That deep desire for health for our son, with no apparent answers to my prayers, was the foundation of my search of scriptures for the promises of prayer. So it hit me hard that now Nancy also had a disease that wouldn't go away.

For several months the only praying that was being done for my children was done by my husband, our family and our loving church community. I couldn't pray for them any more because it seemed obvious God wasn't listening to me. I knew deep in my heart that there can be nothing wrong with God, so something had to be wrong with me. I stopped praying for my children for awhile, but eventually, by the grace and love of God, I was led to begin writing a prayer journal. Out of the depths of my sure knowledge that God is good, and that I must not be, I began to write each day's journal entry as a letter to God. Each entry began, and still does begin, with addressing God as "Dear Lord" and filling in the rest of the prayer with adoration, confession, thanksgiving and supplication. At first my praying echoed my doubts and my feeling of desertion but, after a few years, every time I wrote in the journal I began to feel an excitement, a swelling in my heart that scared me at first. I thought maybe I was getting a little crazy about this "God thing" or that I might be fooling around with something other than God that might possess me, but the mysterious sensation felt good and strongly like an affirmation of God's presence with me and acceptance of me. For many years now I have known for sure it is God's actual Presence, the Spirit who is God. It is the Spirit who is God, who dwells in my heart and responds to me when I address her.

Now I understand that what was happening to me was I was being awakened to the very presence of the Holy Spirit in my innermost being. From this very personal experience I am sure when we say God is far away and our prayers don't reach him it is because we are not open to that presence which is the Holy Spirit within us. The truth is that God is as close to us as our own hearts, our own being. Part of the Holy Spirit's work is to move in each person to bring her into a relationship with the Creator. This is a relationship that draws the person toward being who God intended her to be and toward being a partner in the work of God's Spirit. The work of the Spirit includes filling the universe with life, moving through the events of the world to accomplish good, and dwelling within our reach to lead us to abundant life with God.

Just as the Spirit of God dwells in the heart and mind of each believer so also the Spirit of God acts in the life of the world. A hymn, simply named "Spirit" written by James K. Manley in 1975, expresses beautifully and movingly the activity of God the Spirit in our souls and in the world, in its history and in its future. The refrain describes the nature of the Spirit:

> *Spirit, spirit of gentleness, blow through the wilderness, calling and free,*
> *Spirit, spirit of restlessness, stir me from placidness, wind, wind on the sea.*

The verses and the tune to which they are set describe the activity of the Spirit of God as she moves through history.

> *You moved on the waters, you called to the deep,*
> *Then you coaxed up the mountains from the valleys of sleep,*
> *And over the eons you called to each thing,*
> *Awake from your slumbers and rise on your wings.*

> *You swept through the desert, you stung with the sand,*
> *And you gifted your people with a law and a land,*
> *And when they were blinded with their idols and lies,*
> *Then you spoke through your prophets to open their eyes.*

> *You sang in a stable, You cried from a hill,*
> *Then You whispered in silence when the whole world was still,*
> *And down in the city You called once again*
> *When you blew through Your people on the rush of the wind.*

> *You call from tomorrow, You break ancient schemes,*
> *From the bondage of sorrow the captives dream dreams,*
> *And our women see visions, our men clear their eyes.*
> *With bold new decisions your people arise.*[2]

---

2.   James K. Manley, 1975, *The Presbyterian Hymnal,* (Louisville, KY: Westminster/ John Knox Press, 1990) 319.

The words of this song and the tune to which it is sung tell us of the activity of God, the Holy Spirit, throughout the eons. In the creation story it was the Spirit of God who moved over the face of the waters and brought forth the creation. In the story of the Exodus it was the Spirit of God who led the people through the desert. It was the Spirit who opened the eyes of the prophets and enabled them to speak fearlessly about what they saw. It was the Spirit in the life of Jesus that caused his birth in the stable and his resurrection on Easter morning. It is the Spirit of God that calls to us from the future, a future of hope for all people. The activity of the Spirit is mediated to us through the natural world, through personal and interpersonal relationships, and through human community. Everyone and everything has the potential to be touched by the power of the Spirit.

Within the Judeo-Christian faith the Spirit is recognized to be everywhere, active in all things, "always drawing near and passing by, shaping fresh starts of vitality and freedom."[3] Observing the activity of God is the only way we can come close to knowing God, to naming God. For Christians, divine activity is described in terms of the Trinity. Simply and traditionally stated: God the Father is the Creator and Sustainer of the universe; the Son is the Redeemer of all that has gone astray; and the Holy Spirit is the presence of God active in the world today. The hardest part of thinking about the Trinity is to understand that God's being is not divided into three parts, but rather these are three ways humans experience God's behavior. In three ways the Divine acts in the lives of humans.

In my experience and in that of most Christians, I venture to say, the roles of the first two persons of the Trinity have been clearer than that of the Spirit, which in spite of the way we have just described the Spirit, has always been pretty hazy. The fact that for generations this person of the Trinity was called by such an amorphous name as Holy Ghost and has always been named last, after the Father and the Son, is evidence that we have not known what words to use when we talk about the Spirit.

Vagueness about the Holy Spirit is not only a failing of individual Christians, but rather is also a reflection of what the church has taught, or more accurately not taught, about this person of the Trinity. The history of the formation of the doctrines of the church shows that the Spirit, while it is the first way human beings experience God, was the last to be named divine. The first expression of the Spirit as the third person of the Godhead was not made until the fourth century in the Nicene Creed.

---

3.   Johnson, *She Who Is,* 127.

And we believe in the Holy Spirit, the Lord and Giver of Life, who proceedeth from the Father and the Son, who with the Father and the Son together is worshipped and glorified, who spoke by the prophets.[4]

Even after the church began using this confession, the Spirit did not receive the same attention as was given to the Father and the Son. Some theologians of those early days emphasized the transcendence of God more than the immanence of God, consequently one reason for neglect of the Holy Spirit could be that by the time the theologians had written about and discussed the roles of the Father and the Son in creation and redemption and their relationship to each other there was little time, space or energy left to devote to the person of God who is named last. Even Thomas Aquinas, one of the most important of the classical theologians, wrote in the thirteenth century that the "procession" of God who is love (the Holy Spirit) has no proper name of its own.

Another possible reason for the neglect of the Spirit is that after Martin Luther set in motion the Reformation in 1517, Protestant and Roman Catholic theology took different directions in their interpretation of the Spirit. For Protestants, the Spirit's work came to be that of justifying and sanctifying the life of the individual believer. It was the Spirit's work to "save" individuals. Roman Catholic theology of this time tended in the opposite direction toward institutionalizing the work of the Spirit by tying it to ecclesiastical office and ordained ministry. The Church became the expression of the Spirit which resulted in many functions of the divine Spirit being placed on the pope, the cult of the Blessed Sacrament, or the Virgin Mary. In Roman Catholic theology the progression of the three persons could be expressed in the words: I come to a living faith in the triune God through Christ in His Church.

The Virgin Mary came to be seen as the one who is present to guide and to inspire believers, making her the mediator between a believer and Christ. Mary was also given other functions which biblically belonged to the Spirit such as helper, advocate, defender, consoler, and counselor. Pope Leo XIII (1810-1878 C.E.) wrote that every grace granted to human beings comes in this way: through God to Christ to Mary and then to us. Contemporary Roman Catholic theologians attribute this use of Mary to the undeveloped state of thought about the Spirit in medieval Latin theology.

---

4.   The Constitution of the Presbyterian Church (USA) Part I, Book of Confessions, 1:1-3.

These two developments in the doctrine of the Holy Spirit (the Reformation and the Roman Catholic theology that followed the Council of Trent) have had serious effects on Christian theology:

> The cumulative effect of this rather meager Western pneumatological tradition has been that the full range of the reality and activity of God the Spirit has been virtually lost from much of Christian theological consciousness.[5]

In recent years yet another reason has been proposed for the neglect of the Spirit: the gendered feminine characteristics evoked by female images and metaphors used for the Spirit caused the Spirit to be marginalized just as women were. What happened to women happened to the Holy Spirit. In chapter five where we considered the words *ruah, shekinah and hokma/sophia,* we learned that it is appropriate to speak of the Spirit in metaphors which reflect the image of God in feminine language. In the early years of the church the association of the Spirit with these feminine images was strong and powerful. Rather than dealing with the deep meaning of a feminine presence in God, theologians and the church put aside her femininity. What the Spirit does can certainly be compared to women's work which goes on continuously in home, church and countless social groupings. It is possible that because names for the Spirit were feminine, she was passed over lightly or ignored by those who believed that women were more prone to sin than men and also weaker and less intelligent.

Following the path of Elizabeth Johnson in *She Who Is* we have begun our exploration of the Trinity not with God the person called Father who is always named first, but with a discussion of God the person called Spirit/Sophia who is traditionally named third. There are at least three good reasons for starting the discussion here. First, the presence of the Spirit is one that is attested to by human experience. Second, there is a universal belief among all peoples that there is a spirit which pervades all things. Third, starting with the Spirit makes the discussion more intelligible to contemporary minds.

First, the presence of the Holy Spirit is closely in tune with the human experience of salvation. A person is touched first by the Spirit. The Spirit makes her presence known in effects such as "new life and energy, peace and justice, resistance and liberation, hope against hope, wisdom, courage, and all that goes with love.[6]

---

5.   Johnson, *She Who Is,* 130.
6.   Ibid., 122.

Starting with the Spirit is in keeping with what human beings experience in their daily lives and with the way faith in the Triune God arises—the Spirit moves the heart of a person into faith in the other two. As humans speak about the Trinity, just as when they speak about God, only metaphors are possible and the best metaphors to describe the Trinity are those which convey action, since God is life and energy and love.

> She is life, movement, color, radiance, restorative silence in din. Her power makes all withered sticks and souls green again with the juice of life. She purifies, absolves, strengthens, heals, gathers the perplexed, seeks the lost. She pours the juice of contrition into hardened hearts. She plays music in the soul, being herself the melody of praise and joy. She awakens mighty hope, blowing everywhere the winds of renewal in creation. And this is the mystery of God in whom we live and move and have our being.[7]

Again, I quote Dr. Johnson because her words are so poetic and expressive of the movement of the Trinity.

> If God as primordial origin is pictured as the sun, and God incarnate as a beam of that same light streaming to the earth (Christ the sunbeam), then Spirit is the point of light that actually arrives and affects the earth with warmth and energy. And it is all the one shining light. Again, triune holy mystery may be pictured as an upwelling spring of water, the river that flows outward from this source, and the irrigation channel where the water meets and moistens the earth—again, Spirit. And it is all the one flowing water. Yet again, the triune God can be compared to a flowering plant with its deep, invisible root, its green stem reaching into the world from that root, and its flower (Spirit) which opens to spread beauty and fragrance and to fructify the earth with fruit and seed. And it is all the one living plant.[8]

Elizabeth Johnson draws these images from early Christian thought but they still have power to inspire us as we work with a new language to use to name toward God. What we experience and declare in our lives and what we witness to is the activity of the Spirit. People of faith experience the Spirit as the life of all that is; as the connectedness between people and events; as the spark that inflames hearts to good works, as healing and serenity.

The second reason for approaching the Trinity first from the Spirit is that there always has been in every time and place a universal belief in a divine spirit of

---

7. Ibid., 128.
8. Ibid., 127.

some kind. This Being permeates the world, bringing life to all creation and sustaining life for all creatures both human and nonhuman. In searching for an illustration for this thought I turned again to the book, *One River, Many Wells,* by Matthew Fox. Instead of finding one simple illustration I discovered that the whole book is about the Divine Spirit who is at the heart and core of all of humankind's search for truth, beauty and goodness. True to the title, Fox uses quotes from the religions of the world which show the cosmic presence of the Divine Spirit. These sacred, beautiful, and inspiring words guide one toward a deeper understanding of the work of the Spirit and the universality of her Being.

Third, the Holy Spirit as starting place makes the discussion more intelligible to many contemporary minds who question the existence of God. When we begin with what we know (the Spirit of God moving in our lives) and reason to what we do not know (God eternal in all divine mystery) the need for proving the existence of God is diminished. Our acknowledgment of the activity of God in our life leads to the sure knowledge that God does exist.

One of the great mysteries of God is that God is transcendent and at the same time immanent. God is magnificent, mysterious Creator of all that is at the same time God dwells in the midst of creation. Spirit is the word theology has chosen to describe this aspect of God because it signifies a power that does not arise from human initiative but rather precedes, undergirds and surrounds humans. It describes a relation that makes all else possible: the Creator Spirit at the very heart of the world. Using the word, Spirit, helps describe divine elusiveness and underlines the fact that no human idea can ever define it. We can see this in the cosmic images Scripture uses for Spirit: blowing wind, flowing water, burning fire, light. None of these images has a stable definite shape which can be held onto, but each has an impact on the world it touches. The human world, as well as the natural world, provides analogies for the Spirit. In the Hebrew Scriptures *ruah* engages in many activities that can be spoken of as women's work. *Ruah* (spirit) creates new life, sustains life, repairs what has been damaged, teaches people to be wise. Scripture uses a range of suggestive imagery to speak about these activities. It speaks of them as water that cleanses and refreshes, fire that warms and brightens, cloud that cools and wind that blows free.

The Spirit of God who blows where she will cannot be tied down or confined to any box built by officials or by dogma. Thinking about the Spirit as it is experienced in women's lives does two things: it affirms women's experience and helps us uncover much that has been largely ignored in the approach which begins with the Creator God who is always addressed as male. However, if in our search for a feminine understanding of God we simply say that God has a feminine side as well as a masculine side we will be reinforcing the gender stereotypes of female and male. We will still be saying that men behave in such and such a way and that women behave in a different way, stereotyping both and leaving masculinity in the superior position which has been assigned to it through the ages. God is whole and every time human beings address the Divine we are using a small piece of creation to describe a Being we cannot fully describe. God is one whose image is mirrored equally in male and female. As we examine our classical theological heritage we are seeking understandings of God that adhere to women's experience of the holy and that will lead us toward new language about God.

This search through our classical heritage for an understanding of the Spirit of God that will harmonize with women's experience of God and lead toward new naming of the mystery of God, uncovers many verbs which are appropriate to the task. Of the many such verbs we will look at four: vivify, renew and empower, and grace.

The dictionary definition of *vivify* says it in a nutshell: "to give life to, to make come to life, to animate."[9] It is through the Creator Spirit that the whole universe comes to life and remains alive. This creative God relates:

> ...to the cosmos as well as to the human world, to communities as well as individuals, to new productions of the mind and spirit as well as to new biological life. All creatures receive existence as her gift, she who is named in the Nicene-Constantinopolitan creed giver of life, the vivifier.[10]

In the very beginning "the Spirit of God was moving over the face of the waters" (Gen 1:2). She was there hovering over the chaos as she began to bring order and to create life. However, creation is not a one-time event but rather a continuing activity of the Spirit. Her presence and activity in the cosmos is what keeps everything alive. She is the giver of life and the lover of life. Job said, "The Spirit of God has made me, and the breath of the Almighty gives me life" (Job 33:4).

The Spirit vivifies and she also *renews* and *empowers* life. Psalm 104:30 says "When you send forth your Spirit, they are created; and you renew the face of the ground." The earth and its creatures, human and nonhuman, are always in need of renewal.

---

9. *Webster's New World Dictionary, Second College Edition,* (Simon and Schuster, 1980).
10. Johnson, *She Who Is,* 134.

> Wherever the gift of healing and liberation in however partial a manner reaches the winterized or damaged earth, or peoples crushed by war and injustice, or individual persons weary, harmed, sick, or lost on life's journey, there the new creation in the spirit is happening.[11]

The Spirit *graces* her creation. Up to this point in our discussion we have set her work in the widest ways possible. She gives life. She renews life. She empowers life. Nothing specifically religious has been singled out, although what we have seen her doing is of immeasurable religious significance. She causes the flourishing of the earth, of social structures and of every person's life. However, the world of the specifically religious is also an arena for Spirit-Sophia's presence and work. The offer of the Spirit's grace is universal. Throughout all creation it is the theme of the religions of the world in their narrative and ritual. When we talk about grace we are talking about the Spirit's work of reaching out and drawing all creation toward the holiness of God.

> Above all, prophecy with its strong ethical dimension is a sign of special endowment by her power. Abiding with the people and accompanying them through the vicissitudes of history, even absenting herself in what are experienced as times of dryness and exile, the Spirit creates the covenantal bonds that make Israel the people of God.[12]

The Christian community has its origins in the tradition of the Jewish people and inherits from Judaism a basic understanding of the Spirit. As a result, virtually every New Testament author understands the history and destiny of Jesus-the-Jew-become-Christ, as a Spirit phenomenon. The Spirit is described as active in the infancy narratives, in his baptism, in his temptations, in his preaching and healing, in his solidarity with the poor and outcast, in his suffering and dying on the cross and in his resurrection from the dead. In the entire life, death and resurrection of Jesus Christ, the Spirit is present and active in a singular way to begin the reign of God on earth.

After the resurrection the Spirit descended upon men and women as wind and tongues of flame at the event called Pentecost. The Spirit inspired in these people and all believers since boldness and the desire to preach the gospel. All those who believe in Jesus Christ believe that their community, the church, was created by the Spirit. They believe that it is in and through the Spirit that the risen Lord

---

11. Ibid., 135.
12. Ibid., 139.

remains present with them always and forever. They affirm their belief and their experience in Acts 15:28: "It has seemed good to the Holy Spirit and to us." The biblical narratives of these origins of the Christian church show us that Christian life is not possible apart from the presence and activity of the Spirit who gives the church life and makes her holy. The work of Spirit-Sophia encompasses the breadth, depth, and historical length of the whole world. Throughout history Western theology has searched for terms which would crystallize the meaning of the Spirit of God within a Trinitarian framework and ground her influence in the Ultimate Being.

Classical theology defined Spirit as love and as gift. Spirit as love has been accepted as mutual love—love of the three persons of the Trinity for each other (thus making Love a name for God) and the love that proceeds from the God-head giving life and energy to all of creation. Always this theology maintained that the three persons of the Trinity are equal but at the same time spoke of the Spirit as love proceeding. In Eastern theology the Spirit proceeded from the Father. In the West the Spirit proceeded from the Father and the Son. In both cases the idea of "proceeding from" gives the impression, the appearance that the Spirit is of lesser importance.

Traditionally, when someone writes or speaks about the Trinity she considers the three in the order of Father, Son and Holy Spirit. A positive aspect of this ordering of the three persons is that it seems logical chronologically to start with God the Father as Creator, proceed to the Son of God as Redeemer, then to the Holy Spirit as the Spirit of Christ still and always dwelling among us in the absence of the Lord's physical body.

A downside to the traditional approach is that, under the influence of hierarchical thinking, the ordering becomes an ordering from above with God at the top, Jesus in the middle and the Spirit at the bottom. It suggests and supports the idea that the three persons of the Trinity are named in the order of their importance. This arrangement of the three then becomes a power structure that leads to the approval of hierarchical ratings in human society.

Along with calling Spirit love the classical theologians called her "gift." The love that is the Godhead is also gift to her creation. "God's love has been poured into our hearts through the Holy Spirit which has been given to us" (Rom. 5:5). Speaking of the spirit as the power of mutual love proceeding has strong likenesses to the model of relationship that is prized by feminists.

> ...Love is the moving power of life, that which drives everything that is toward everything else that is. When love is mutual it signifies a respect, a priz-

ing, and a bondedness that subvert the potential for domination inherent in peoples' concrete differences. Spoken of in terms of mutual love proceeding, God who is Spirit cannot be used to legitimize patriarchal structures but signals a migration toward reciprocity in community as the highest good. As the creative dynamic of mutual love, the Spirit vitally moves, attracts, impels, connects and sets up a solidarity of reciprocal, freeing relation throughout the whole world as well as between herself and creation.[13]

When we understand the dynamic freedom of the Spirit in all that she does and at the same time name her as gift, we are able to see God as a mystery of self-giving who liberally graces all creation, not because she has to but freely because that is her nature. John 3:8 says she blows where she will, a fitting image for the freedom of the giver who is herself the gift. She models for women and men alike the beauty of mature self-giving which comes not from pressure exerted by the expectations of other people, but from simply being free to give oneself.

Hopefully, by now we are able more comfortably to consider feminine names for the Spirit, metaphors that describe Spirit-Sophia in female terms. Some names which are fitting for Spirit-Sophia are friend, sister, mother and grandmother. The idea of friend helps make concrete the abstract idea of love and gift. Classical theology talked about God in terms of friend, but didn't value it as an important way to speak of God. Thomas Aquinas developed the analogy of human friendship when he said that by the Holy Spirit we are established as friends of God. However, he did not establish that the relationship is reciprocal: we are friends of God and God is a friend to us. God's power and action described as Spirit, show us a way of relating to God and God to us that is mutual, describing full friendship from God's side as well as from the human side. All that is good and rich and deep and mutually fulfilling about friendship can be applied to God's relationship to creation as well as human relationship to God. As friend of the world, Spirit shows humans that they are never alone in their personal or global anxieties but that they are supported and directed by a Friend who has similar cares.

We can further define the model of friend when we use the image of sister. Sisterhood is a concept prized by feminists. At its best the relationship of sisters is one of equality and solidarity on a peer level, not one over the other. Having been blessed with three sisters, I know that we can be comfortable and joyful with each other or we can be at odds, but always we uphold, support and defend one another

---

13. Ibid., 143.

Women's relationship to their mothers and grandmothers may also help us name the Spirit by those names. The Spirit's actions of vivifying, renewing and gracing can be spoken of in terms of mother and grandmother. In these images—friend, sister, mother, grandmother—we see that the Spirit builds relationships of solidarity not polarity between God and human beings, between human beings, between human beings and the earth.

8

Jesus-Sophia

○ ○

...the Son of Man came eating and drinking, and they say, 'Look, a glutton and a drunkard, a friend of tax collectors and sinners!' Yet wisdom is vindicated by her deeds. (Matthew 11:19)

Christian faith is grounded on the experience that God who is Spirit at work in the tragic and beautiful world to vivify and renew all creatures through the gracious power of her indwelling, liberating love, is present yet again through the very particular history of one human being, Jesus of Nazareth. [1]

A few years ago there appeared in shopping malls and stores pictures which made good gift items because they were so new no one had any. The pictures appeared to be only bright and lovely colors in random patterns, however what appeared to be just an interesting arrangement of colors and shapes actually concealed a three dimensional scene. In order to see the picture that was portrayed in three dimensions by the arrangement of colors a person had to stare unblinkingly at the picture until it came into focus. Some people could do it and some couldn't. Some could do it easily and some had to stare at it until they had sore eyes and a headache and sometimes even then it did not come into focus. Oftentimes the picture would start to come into focus and then dissolve back into the colors.

As I have struggled to understand Jesus as Sophia, I have experienced something akin to the activity of staring at those seemingly indecipherable colors until, for instance, a beautiful picture of an eagle in flight came into focus. At first all I

1.　Ibid., 150.

could see were the colors and the apparent arrangement of them, just as until recently, all I could see in my understanding of Jesus was the beauty of his life and love and ministry in the old familiar shapes I was taught. As I stared at the picture of Jesus through eyes opened by Christian feminist theology, I began to realize that what we see in the traditional understanding of Jesus is not all there is. I began to realize that there is more to Jesus, God who became human, than I had been taught and more than is being taught and believed today. Hidden in what I have always believed about Christ is Jesus-Sophia.

It has taken me years of staring at and concentrating on the concept of Jesus-Sophia to come to the point where it now seems clearer—not easy to hold on to, but clearer. And it is beautiful! Like those pictures it is fleeting—sometimes I've got it and sometimes I don't. In order to know Jesus better, which is a goal of the Christian believer, it is important not to give up but to keep trying to see Jesus in this rich, new way until you can do it.

The importance of this effort lies in the fact that seeing Jesus as Sophia opens up whole new vistas of faith for women and men, most especially for those who have been relegated to positions of inferiority in home, in church and in society. Shining the spotlight on Jesus-Sophia and his life and teaching draws attention to and focuses on what has always been there: that Jesus' willingness to serve and to suffer for others is one of the characteristic modes of behavior for women through all the generations in the history of the world.

We profess that Jesus is fully human and fully divine. However, if we concentrate only on his humanity as male we rule out the possibility that the feminine Spirit-Sophia also resides in him. As is common among believers, even though I accepted the doctrine of Jesus' full humanity and full divinity, I continued to live mainly with the fully human part as the basis of my faith, which worked for me until I began this feminist journey. It is naturally easy to relate to Jesus, the human male, because, though sinless, he was just like us: experiencing sorrow, tiredness, hunger, frustration, and grief as well as joy, contentment, love and compassion. It is not enough to relate to Jesus as purely human because we profess that Jesus the Christ was God himself incarnate. As we grow into faith and knowledge that Sophia is an acceptable and even desirable name for God the potential is also there to accept that Jesus, God Incarnate, can equally as well be called Jesus, Sophia Incarnate.

> According to the witness of Scripture, Jesus is a genuine Spirit-phenomenon, conceived, inspired, sent, hovered over, guided, and raised from the dead by her power. In its etymological and historical context, the early Christian con-

fession that Jesus is the Christ means precisely this, that he is the Messiah, the anointed one, the one anointed by the Spirit. Through his human history the Spirit who pervades the universe becomes concretely present in a small bit of it; Sophia pitches her tent in the midst of the world; the Shekinah dwells among the suffering people in a new way. In a word, Jesus is Emmanuel, God with us.[2]

This is the good news! God is not some distant figure who looks down upon creation watching what is happening or even guiding human actions like a master player at a chess board. God is Spirit-Sophia, who dwells in the midst of her creation relating to her human creatures in love and compassion, wanting them to relate to her and all other creatures—human and nonhuman—in love and compassion. Sophia is the Spirit who created all that is. She loves and dwells within all that is. The Gospels tell us that because of the way Jesus lived his life, good news is preached to persons who are poor, disrespected, oppressed, struggling, victimized, the majority of whom are women and children. Because of the Spirit's filling of the man Jesus, humankind has been given clear directions for how to value life and give meaning to it.

The fact that the Savior of the world came as a man has been used to minimize the nature and the importance of women, which is contrary to anything Jesus said or did. However, in each new age, in trying to say who Jesus was (Christology) the church mirrored the times in which it lived, the worldview of the people around it. Of all the doctrines of the Church, Christology is the doctrine most used to suppress and exclude women. This came about in part because the early Church moved from a community wherein all its members were valued equally to one that took on the form of the patriarchal household and the hierarchical state by which the Greco-Roman world was ordered. In this cultural structure the man was the head of the household just as the emperor was the head of the nation.

Jesus, who served as a humble servant of all, came to be viewed as the supreme model of headship and cosmic order, the ruling king of glory. Accordingly, it was his reign over all that set up and sustained the earthly authority of the head of the family, of the Empire and of the Church. Obedience to the earthly authorities was seen as obedience to Christ. Likewise disobedience to them was considered disobedience to Christ. This view of Jesus the Christ is used as justification for the exclusion of women from leadership and results in their subjection to male authority. The bottom line is,

---

2.   Ibid., 150.

> …when Jesus' maleness, which belongs to his historical identity, is interpreted to be essential to his redeeming christic function and identity, then the Christ serves as a religious tool for maligning and excluding women.[3]

Jesus' maleness is not in question here. It is a historical fact that he was a man, just as it is a historical fact that he was a Jew, a carpenter, a rabbi. His historical identity is not the problem. The problem is that the church took one aspect of his earthly existence and made it the norm for authority in family, church and nation, with two major results that are like two sides of the same coin. One side of the coin implies that since Jesus was a male then God's essential being must be male. God is the patriarch above all patriarchs. John's gospel reinforces the maleness of God in Jesus Christ with the use of the word *logos* which was connected with the male principle in Greek philosophy.

The second major result, the flip side of the coin, is that certain perceptions about maleness are created. It strengthens the belief that a particular honor, dignity, and normativity characterize the male sex because it was chosen by God himself when he came into this world as a human being. The way this reasoning goes is that since God chose to be incarnated as a man, God must see more value in maleness than in femaleness.

Such reasoning leads many to the conclusion that men are like God/Jesus in ways which go far beyond what is possible for women. Roman Catholics use this argument against the ordination of women, saying that since Jesus was a male therefore priests must be male. The same argument is part of the ground for the debates that Protestant men, and strangely enough some women, raise when women's ordination is discussed in Protestant circles. There it is said females are not suited for this sacred and very demanding role. Besides carrying the sinfulness of Eve in their very being, women are neither as emotionally strong nor intellectually wise as men are so they are unfit to bring the Gospel to people or to officiate at the sacraments. Jesus was a man; therefore God is male; therefore women are excluded from leadership in the church but are given support roles—a scenario which echoes society itself.

In any theology the thinker starts with herself and how she sees God. Therefore, for women to theologize from a male point of view is to sell out on their being equal with men in the image of God. Feminist theologians have identified three ways of thinking about the relationship of male and female. The first, dualistic anthropology, is the way human beings are widely defined at the present time. It maintains that men and women are totally different in nature and that

---

3.   Ibid., 151.

men are superior to women. Expressed in the practice of the Christian faith this means that salvation comes only through the male Jesus and, therefore, only through male clergy. Thus it follows that salvation must come through men to women. The Church of the Latter Day Saints (Mormons) states very clearly that a woman acquires a place in heaven only by her husband's sponsorship. While other branches of Christianity would not say it so boldly, their practice has also been that women are saved through their relationship to a male God represented by male leadership which includes their husbands, fathers or sons.

The second anthropological stance is that developed by feminist advocates in the beginning of such debate. It is that of a single nature which views sexual difference as only important for reproduction. This view holds that sexual differences do not determine who a person is but rather that each individual is free to develop the best of traditional masculine or feminine characteristics as they search for wholeness. The stress is on similarity rather than on difference to the extent that real differences are largely ignored. This view is criticized because it tends to hold out a single human ideal and is destructive of the rich variety of humanity expressed through human sexuality.

It would seem that the choice is between only two views: either two separate types of human nature or unisex. But there is a way beyond these two, neither of which accurately portray human realities. It is the idea of one human nature that is celebrated in an interdependence of multiple differences. This view looks toward a diversity of ways of being human. The stories, historical and fictional, which we have been told have almost always fit into the category of dualistic anthropology, that is, men and women are so totally different from each other that we can even talk about "the battle of the sexes." It is commonplace to attack and make jokes about weaknesses in each other as though the trait attacked belonged exclusively to one sex or the other.

Since retiring to Arizona I have been reading histories of the Southwest and have discovered, much to my amazement and delight, that there were women who were stage coach drivers, ranchers, and miners. We could understand the nature of male and female better if we could see them in a more holistic context not bound by gender stereotypes. We need to see that sexuality is not the only context in which to view people.

It is shortsighted to single out sexuality as always and everywhere more fundamental to concrete historical experience than any of the other constants. Age, race, period in history, bodily handicap, social location, and other essential aspects of concrete historical existence are at least as important in determining one's identity as sex. Focusing on sexuality to the exclusion of other equally constitutive elements is the equivalent of using a microscope on this one key factor of human life when what is needed is a telescope to take in the galaxies of rich human difference. In a multipolar model, sexuality is integrated into a holistic vision of human persons instead of being made the touchstone of personal identity and thus distorted.[4]

This model of multiple differences moves us beyond the ideas of sexual dualism versus unisex to the celebration of diversity as completely normal. It is easy to see how great freedom could result from this multipolar anthropology. Individuals could be who they were created to be, and do what they are best suited to do, without censure or ridicule. A man could teach preschoolers without being looked down on as being less of a man than a man who teaches high school students. A woman could spend her days in the work place without feeling guilty because she has been taught that her only real value is in serving her husband and children at home. What needs to be done to achieve this freedom for women and men is to look at Christ in a new way, which is to look at Jesus' maleness as intrinsically important for who he was in history but not as required for his identity as the Christ. When we look at Christ we are looking at God whose image is male and female.

When a little girl asks the question, "Why didn't God send his daughter instead of his son?" there are answers to her question. One is that God the Parent sent the child as a male to teach and model a reversal of values. Jesus taught that the first shall be last, that it is better to serve than to be served, to give than to receive. Jesus was turning the tables and it needed to be a man who did it because, in hearing his message, men were being called to a dramatic reversal of understanding and behavior.

Women, girls and slaves were the servants, men, as a class, were not. As Jesus the man modeled his message he taught that righteousness is measured by service to others. Women were already servants to fathers, husbands and sons, so a daughter-Messiah would have been shrugged off as a shrewish woman who didn't appreciate her protected role in life. Jesus came to teach men and boys also to be servants, to put others first. Whenever I say or write something like that I always feel like a disgruntled woman and have to add that not all women are perfectly meek and obedient nor are all men totally bossy and controlling. But it is possible and necessary to make blanket assessments of the sexes which are accurately descriptive of women-as-a-group and men-as-a group since we need to understand how things are before we can change them.

---

4.   Ibid., 156.

As a man Jesus could show men and women the value of characteristics that are normally attributed to women: compassion, humility, cooperation, selflessness. Miriam Therese Winter suggests that God became flesh as a male in order to:

> ...witness to the value of the feminine, to teach men, through Jesus that affirming the feminine is compatible with being a man, to teach us all, women and men, that true mutuality, true equality, is the core of the gospel's good news.[5]

Another answer to a little girl's question of why God sent Jesus as a son instead of as a daughter is that it would have been impossible for a woman to spread the message as widely as a man could. It was against Jewish law for a woman in Jesus' time to speak in public or even to speak privately with men who were not her husband or relatives. The extent of a woman's influence would have been within her own household and with women friends whom she would meet at the well or some other place where women did their work.

Jesus' being a man in human form did not erase his being God, male and female. Even though Jesus was a man physically, his being God makes it possible to see Christ as feminine as well as seeing him as the man he was. The earliest Christian hymns proclaim that Christ was pre-existent in the image of Divine Sophia. The writer of Hebrews says in the opening verses that God created the world through Christ and that he reflects the glory of God. The "glory of God" to the Jewish people was called *Shekinah*, a female being. This name is used in rabbinic writings as a synonym for divine presence among the people. As the rabbis read and taught Israel's history they saw God's presence in the form of female presence, the Shekinah. Since Jesus' disciples and many other of the first Christians came from the Jewish faith, the composers and first singers of the early hymns would quite naturally see the risen Jesus as Shekinah, the Divine One who dwells with her people. These hymns or fragments of hymns can be found in John 1:1-18; Ephesians 2:14-16; Philippians 2:6-11; I Timothy 3:16; I Peter 3:18-22 and possibly I John 1:1-3. Naming Jesus Sophia was not confined to the singing of the early church, but was also present in Paul's preaching as seen in I Corinthians 1:10-31 (especially vss. 27 & 30), I Corinthians 2:6-13 and in the Pauline tradition in Colossians

---

5.   Miriam Therese Winter, *WomanPrayer, WomanSong*, (Bloomington, IN, Meyer-Stone Books, 1987) 7.

1:15-29. It is possible that the Sophia/Logos tradition may also be observed in Hebrews 1:1-4.[6]

In November of 1993 more than 2,000 women and men from around the world gathered in Minneapolis, Minnesota for a global theological colloquium, which was organized locally in response to the World Council of Churches' Ecumenical Decade: Churches in Solidarity with Women (1988-1998). The very theme of the conference, *RE-IMAGINING...God...Community...The Church,* caused much conflict because some people saw it as an exercise in heresy. It was reported that the participants were worshipping Sophia which was perceived as praying to a goddess. Many and varied accusations were made and many people, presenters and participants alike, were deeply wounded spiritually and emotionally; they were attacked and rejected in their church communities. In listening to the tapes of all the speeches and much of the worship, I learned that not as much was made of Sophia in the conference itself as was made of her in the raging controversy that ensued. What was evident, and what was probably as frightening as anything to the powers that be, was that women were finding a voice with which to speak their history, their feelings and their hopes. The church is in need of more re-imagining conferences in order to think and speak about God who is as fully present in women's lives as in men's.

Even if Sophia had been the center of worship and adoration in this gathering it would not necessarily have been heresy, because Sophia was worshipped by the Jews in Jesus' time and consequently by the first Christians, whose roots were in Judaism. In her book, *In Search of the Christ-Sophia,* Jann Aldredge-Clanton writes:

> Through applying wisdom imagery to Christ, these New Testament hymns stress the continuity between the person of Christ and God's creative, revelatory, and redemptive action. Christ alone so embodies Sophia that what can be said of Sophia can be said of Christ. In the early church the application of Sophia categories to Christ went hand-in-hand with the concept of the pre-existence of Christ.[7]

---

6. The texts cited here are from the website of Faith Futures Foundation which in their own words is "a grassroots response to a widely perceived need for new ways to express and explore the sacred knowledge that we have inherited from the past through our religions and spiritual traditions." An advisor in the foundation is Marcus Borg, author of *Reading the Bible Again for the First Time.*

7. Jann Aldredge Clanton, *In Search of the Christ-Sophia,* An Inclusive Christology for Liberating Christians, (Mystic CT, Twenty-Third Publications, 1995) 18.

The accusations, fuss, and anger over using the word *Sophia* stem in part from a lack of knowledge about the Wisdom literature in the Bible. This is especially a problem for Protestants since, unlike Roman Catholics, they do not accept as Scripture the apocryphal books, which are where much Wisdom (Sophia) literature is found. The Apocryphal books and the New Testament both point to Jesus as Sophia in the flesh. Sophia who dwelt with God before creation, who was the moving Spirit throughout the world, became incarnate in Jesus Christ. Jesus is Sophia incarnate.

Not only does using the female gender symbolism cast Jesus into an inclusive framework with regard to his relationships with human beings and with God, it removes the male emphasis which so quickly turns to androcentrism.[8] Using feminine terminology also evokes Sophia's characteristic gracious goodness, life-giving creativity, and passion for justice as key teaching tools for Christians as they carry out their mission of communicating the good news of Jesus Christ to a world filled with cruelty and injustice.

The connection between Jesus and Wisdom/Sophia is emphasized in the Gospel of Matthew when he writes: "Yet wisdom is vindicated by her deeds" (Mt 11:19). In this passage Matthew reports that Jesus was criticized for going about doing what Sophia has always done and still does and what Jesus invites others to join with him in doing. He walks Sophia's paths of justice and peace. Like her, he:

> ...delights in being with people: joy, insight, and a sure way to God are found in his company. Again and again in imaginative parables, compassionate healings, startling exorcisms, and festive meals he spells out the reality of the gracious goodness and renewing power of Sophia-God drawing near. He addresses her, in all trust, as Abba; he also likens her to a shepherd searching for a lost sheep, a woman looking for her lost coin, a father forgiving his wayward child, a bakerwoman kneading yeast into dough, a mother giving birth.[9]

Differing views on why Jesus died on the cross are held by various Christian communities, but it is apparent that the way Jesus lived his life and what he taught were enough for the authorities to want him dead. All that he said and did flew in the face of the power structures of his day. The powers of the Temple and

---

8.   Androcentrism is the name commonly given to the way of thinking and acting that "takes the characteristics of ruling men to be normative for all people." (Johnson, *She Who Is*, 24) Women, children and men who do not fit this pattern are considered to be inferior.

9.   Johnson, *She Who Is*, 157.

of Rome could not tolerate a teacher who said to love your neighbor as yourself, to turn the other cheek, to cherish things of the spirit more than the things of the world. His teaching that the first shall be last and the last shall be first had to be a thorn in the sides of those who were obviously first in society. Jesus' way of being as Sophia incarnate was a threat to all those who were the beneficiaries of a male dominated society: the Pharisees, Sadducees, scribes and Roman rulers. So they made plans to be rid of him and carried out those plans by crucifying him. They rejected the love, compassion and inclusive call of Sophia, and killed Jesus who was one in a long line of Sophia's murdered prophets. People who accept and act on this message of Jesus/Sophia were and still are a threat to the powers that control and personally benefit from that control.

He was hated, mocked, tortured, and killed because his life and words taught that the way things were had to be changed. After his death and resurrection Sophia, pure, benevolent, people-loving Spirit, was poured out not only on the circle of disciples at Pentecost in that time and in that place, but continues to be poured out on all people as a pledge of Christ's continuing presence with believers. Sophia promises a new future to all who are poor, hungry, bereaved, hated and excluded.

We should note that at the moment of final crisis in Jesus' life women appear boldly in the narrative. All through the Gospels are stories of the love of women for Jesus and their faithful responses to his message. These were not love "affairs." They were the response of marginalized women to one in whom they could see themselves, to one who valued what they valued and who acted with compassion that was common to their nature. We read in Mark 15:41 that Mary Magdalene, Mary the mother of James the younger and of Joses, Salome and many other women disciples were at the foot of the cross during his dying just as they had been by his side during his ministry. Mark, the first of the Gospels to be written, portrays women as the connection between the ministry, and the death, burial and resurrection of Jesus.

> Near or far they keep vigil at the cross, standing in a solidarity with this vilified victim that gives powerful witness to women's courage of relation throughout the ages. Their presence is a sacrament of God's own fidelity to the dying Jesus, their faithful friendship a witness to the hope that he is not totally abandoned. Not in hiding like others of their circle, they know the path to the tomb. Grieving, but on the way to do what needs to be done, they are the first to encounter the risen Christ, to recognize him, to be charged with the mission to tell the good news to those in hiding. This they do: "Now it was Mary Magdalene, Joanna, Mary the mother of James and

the women with them who told this to the apostles" (Lk 24:10), persisting despite ridicule and unbelief.[10]

The picture of Jesus as Sophia is still hard for me to see sometimes, just as the figures that are hidden behind the jumble of colors in the novelty pictures were hard to see. But when I am able to do it, the Jesus I have loved as a friend and comforter and guide since I was a little girl becomes even dearer than those words convey. Jesus/Sophia shows me that God values me, a woman, equally as much as he values men. Learning, as an "outsider", about the man Jesus and the male disciples didn't stop me from loving and following him all these years. In fact, he was the one who showed me, a woman, how to live my life—not as a man like the man Jesus—but as a person who relates to others in love, understanding and compassion. He taught me to serve others and to give of myself when I am needed. He taught me to be like Sophia. Now seeing the feminine in my Lord and Savior not only gives me a truer picture of the fullness of God, but it also helps me know that I, a woman, am a worthwhile and acceptable representation of God, and I can rejoice in the fact that the man Jesus did so much in feminine ways.

Luke tells us (Acts 17:6) that the people of Thessalonica accused the Christians of turning the world upside down. Naming Jesus Sophia would turn family, church and political systems upside down. If Sophia were better understood and Jesus were to be called Sophia we would not only have a new way of naming God, but that new naming would produce more inclusivity and compassion in our world which is so desperately in need of both of those graces.

---

10. Ibid., 159.

9

Mother-Sophia

o o o o o o o o o o o o o o o o o o o o o o o o o o o o o o o o o o

From whose womb did the ice come forth, and who has given birth to the hoarfrost of heaven? (Job 38:29)

For a long time I [God] have held my peace, I have kept still and restrained myself; now I will cry out like a woman in travail, I will gasp and pant. (Isaiah 42:14)

All creatures are siblings from the same womb, the brood of the one Mother of the universe who dwells in bright darkness. In her, as once literally in our own mother, we live and move and have our being, being indeed her offspring (Acts 17:28). [1]

In an adult class I was teaching years ago there was a young father whose deep dedication to Christ showed in his conversation, in his deeds and in his desire for his children to know Jesus and to commit their lives to him. He was of a conservative nature, but not overbearing or judgmental. He sometimes taught the class when I was away and did an excellent job of it. I was too new in feminist theology to be very forceful about it when I taught, so I am sure my feminist leanings had only affected Jeff and the class as a whole only minimally, if at all.

One Sunday morning when we were talking about the nature of God this young father expressed his conviction that God has to be like a mother, because he acts like a mother. Jeff said that when his kids repeatedly do something he has told them not to do he wants to say "That's it! You've had your chance. You're

---

1.   Ibid., 179.

out of here!" But over and over again his wife would give them another chance to do it right. "God has to be like a mother," he said in front of the whole class.

Jeff was thinking of God as a mother from his experience of being a father. The best we as mortals can do is to think of God in terms of our own experience of the divine. We see how God works in our lives and in the lives of others, and in the life and history of the world. That is how we know what to call God, how to name God. Jeff probably would object to the feminine names for God we have been considering, but he certainly did recognize that in at least one respect his wife was more like the Divine One than he was.

Jeff is one of the heirs in a long line of Biblical witnesses who found in the activities of motherhood vibrant metaphors with which to describe God. It is clear from careful Bible study that female symbols for God are taken from many aspects of life and creation not limited to the relationship and role of mothering, but that the metaphor of mother is vitally important and uniquely female. The Bible frequently uses verbs that are unique to motherhood such as bearing, birthing, nursing, and rearing. In passages scattered throughout the Hebrew Scriptures these different aspects of mothering become metaphors for the way God relates to the world.

Deuteronomy 32:18 uses an inanimate object, a rock, to describe God as the one who begot the hearer, but then in the parallel line the verse says: "…you forgot the God who gave you birth." Since giving birth is possible only for females, this is most certainly an image of God as mother. The fact that we can say God gives birth, while at the same time refuse to call her mother, is one of the tricks the power of patriarchy plays on us. In order to retain its power, patriarchy must put its own spin on words and ideas which if expressed as they really are, would upset the whole power system. A male giving birth defies logic; yet it is accepted as a reality for God, who is always seen as male. This twisting of a natural fact is a way to maintain the superiority of the masculine.

Numbers 11:12-13 describes a scene during the Exodus when the Hebrew people were whining, the anger of YHWH was blazing, and Moses was caught in the middle. The text tells us how Moses was feeling. As he was wont to do, Moses talked to God like we would talk to a friend. He asked why YAHWEH gave him the burden of these people: was it I, Moses, who conceived these people and gave birth to them that I should carry them into the promised land as a nurse carries a sucking child? In those days when a midwife delivered a baby, she would lay it on the new mother's breast so it could be fed and warmed. In this event in Moses' life the best analogies he could think of to describe God's relationship to these people were those of midwife and mother. It would seem from this story that Moses felt comfortable likening God to a woman.

The prophet Isaiah also spoke of God in metaphors which show that neither sex nor a name by itself can describe all God is. In Isaiah 42:13-14, the prophet used male and female metaphors side by side in his depiction of God. God is described as a mighty man who goes forth like a man of war stirring up his fury, yelling and shouting to scare his enemies (vs.:13). Immediately after this expression of fury and promise of destruction on the part of the Divine, God's love is described as being like a mother's suffering (vs.14). God, after keeping it bottled up inside for a long time, spoke her agony over her wayward people by saying, "I will cry out like a woman in travail, I will gasp and pant." Isaiah says God will lay waste to creation and will turn the rough places into level ground, but like a mother she will not forsake her people.[2]

There is a deeply rooted connection in the Hebrew Scriptures between God and the womb. In a number of passages in the Old Testament this connection of God with woman's womb is used as an analogy to better understand God. The Psalmist called God a midwife in 22:9-10, saying it is God who assisted in his birth. It was God who caught him as he came from his mother's womb and who laid him on his mother's breasts where he would be safe. The connection of God with woman's womb is a well-chosen analogy leading to a richer understanding of the nature of God.

The theme of God as mother appears again when Isaiah writes, "As a mother comforts her child, so I will comfort you. You shall be comforted in Jerusalem" (66:13). Who among us has not run to her mother for comfort that no one else could give. It was pure comfort without judgment or advice. That is how God comforts us—without blame and without telling us what we should have done. This is not to say that judgment and advice are not important but they have their time and place sometimes separate from the act of comforting.

Another passage in Isaiah 49:15 says, "Can a woman forget her nursing child, or show no compassion for the child of her womb. Even these may forget, yet I will not forget you." A woman, who for one reason or another gives up for adoption or aborts a baby, does not forget that child. Even if neglect and abandonment should happen with a human mother, forgetfulness such as that will never

---

2. In learning this new language it becomes confusing to choose the right pronouns. Mixing masculine and feminine pronouns referring to the same antecedent in the sentence is grammatically incorrect. Furthermore, it reinforces gender stereotypes that say men are more insensitive and women are more compassionate. My rationale for using the mixed pronouns is to show how Isaiah saw God's activity.

happen with God towards us. We can call God mother in the best sense of the word, but God is more than Mother just as she is more than Father.

Phyllis Trible, a Biblical scholar at Union Theological Seminary in New York City, emphasizes that the Hebrew word for woman's womb and the word for compassion are related and both are further related to the verb "to show mercy" and to the adjective "merciful."

> In its singular form the noun *rehem* means "womb" or "uterus." In the plural *rehamin*, this concrete meaning expands to the abstractions of compassion, mercy and love....Accordingly, our metaphor lies in the semantic movement from a physical organ of the female body to a psychic mode of being.[3]

The metaphor moves us from the womb which we know to a way of acting which we want to employ. Compassionate care defines this sentiment which can be seen in men as well as women. All of us can name men we know who have this kind of motherly/womanly love for others. A biblical example is Joseph in Genesis 43:30 who is said to have "womb love" for his brother Benjamin. But it is basically a woman's love for the child of her womb that gives the word compassion its meaning.

> Accordingly, when God is spoken of as merciful, the semantic tenor of the word indicates that the womb is trembling, yearning for the child, grieved at the pain. What is being showered upon the wayward is God's womb-love, divine love for the child of God's womb. "I will truly show motherly compassion upon him" (Jer 31:20). The human experience of giving birth, with its physical and psychic relations, is an analogy that hints at the unfathomable depths of divine love.[4]

Women's bodies bear, nourish and deliver new persons into life. The traditional structure of society has most often charged women with the responsibility to nurture and raise children into maturity. Therefore, words about God as mother carry a unique power to express the human relationship to the divine mystery who conceives and cares for everything.

So what happened to these rich metaphors which showed us the motherly God? Not only are these names for God ignored, but anyone who points them out and begins to call God mother or to use feminine pronouns for her is considered by many people to be at best a nit-picker or at worst a heretic. The creeds

---

3.   Phyllis Trible, *God and the Rhetoric of Sexuality*, (Philadelphia, Fortress, 1978) 33.
4.   Johnson, *She Who Is*, 101.

which have been repeated week after week, year after year, century after century in Christian worship, have ingrained in us the image of the One, all powerful Father who made and rules the world.

The use of the word father for God has become so literalized that we have come to believe that God in his essential being is a father. However, the use of the words father or mother is a metaphor—a way to move in understanding from what we know to what we do not know. It tells us not who God is but how God behaves, how God acts toward us. Therefore if we know God to be acting toward us as a mother, it is appropriate, and indeed helpful, to our spiritual growth to speak of God as our Mother. Like all analogies, all names for God including the name father or mother indicate what God is like, but it must be remembered that God is also unlike that name and is more than that name.

The disappearance of female analogies for God and the literalizing of the masculine for God were not accidental. Even though it was gradual it was intentional When patriarchy emerged as the accepted social structure within the Christian community, the mother image was actively erased from the list of images that were acceptable.

During the first and second centuries of Christianity there was much diversity of thought about the meaning of Christ and how he should be served and worshipped. Since the believers commonly met in house churches which had very little connection to one another, each group developed its own beliefs and practices. Evidence from the early years of this period points toward a recognition and valuing of women. However, as the church grew and a variety of theological ideas surfaced, church leaders began to worry that what they deemed the "real truth" would be lost or distorted. This concern contributed to the perceived need for strong "ruling" leadership which, in Roman society, could be exercised only by men.

When Ignatius, bishop of Antioch, in Syria, was arrested (c. 110 C.E.) and sent by ship to Rome for trial and execution he spent his time writing letters to the churches that were related to his home church in Antioch and to the Christians in Rome.

> Ignatius urged these and all other Christians to stand together under persecution and to maintain unanimous loyalty to the clergy, which he envisioned as a threefold hierarchy of bishop, priests, and deacons who ruled each church "in God's place," and who maintained communication among Christians scattered throughout the world.[5]

5. Elaine Pagels, *Adam, Eve, and the Serpent, (New York, Random House, 1988), 57.*

Second-century Roman society in general believed women were not competent to be leaders; thus it followed that the church adopted the same patriarchal structure. Along with the need for leadership and organization to help the believers stand strong in their faith was the compulsion to decide which beliefs were true and which were not. One system of belief was declared "orthodox" and it began to rewrite:

> ...Christian memory to make it [orthodoxy]appear to have been the sole original form of the Christian movement and making other varieties of Christianity appear secondary deviations (heresies) from an original norm. The "myth of orthodoxy" begins to be shaped by leaders such as Tertullian and Irenaeus in the late second century, as they identify this emerging patriarchal and clerical Christianity with the original "apostolic" faith passed down through an established succession of leaders (bishops) from the apostles who possess the original faith, preserved in the teachings, Scriptures, and practices of the churches led by the apostolic successors.[6]

What human beings think religiously and what is practiced in society unavoidably influence each other so that in this case the church was moved to accept an all-male hierarchical priesthood which in turn necessitated exclusively ruling male images for God. Reading the Gnostic Gospels shows that the maternal imagery did not go down without a struggle, but it did lose out as a consequence of the suppression of the ministry of women in the second century.

For a thousand years women were almost totally shut out of roles in the church. Then along came Thomas Aquinas, who closed the case against using maternal images for God. He incorporated the biology of Aristotle into his theological understanding of the nature of human beings.

> According to Aristotle, in the act of conceiving life, the male is the active partner who provides the vital form and originating movement, while the female is the passive partner providing the inert matter that receives the form. The resulting child is a creation of male energy working on inactive female matter. The two are radical opposites, the man being a vigorous actor and the woman comparable to a lifeless object.[7]

---

6.   Rosemary Radford Ruether, *Women and Redemption, A Theological History,* (Minneapolis, Fortress Press, 1998), 50.

7.   Johnson, *She Who Is,* 174.

The man is active; the woman is passive. This led Aristotle to say, and Aquinas to believe, that a child is formed from both male and female only in the sense in which a bed is formed from the carpenter (the man) and the wood (the woman). As a result, it was reasoned that God cannot be like a woman, cannot be named by feminine names, because it would be an insult to God to say that God is passive when in reality he is the active source of all creation.

This ancient idea of how a child is conceived has long been disproved, but the same philosophical evaluation of women remains. Such flawed and disproved biology is the implicit premise underlying the statements of men theologians and officials of the church who assign women certain preordained "roles" according to this accepted order of nature. Carl Jung, a Swiss psychiatrist and one of the founders of modern depth psychology, furthered the idea of feminine inferiority when he assessed the feminine anima, as void, waiting and darkness. This reason—God cannot be weak and passive—for excluding feminine names for God is being challenged by the activities of women and men in the world today. We must always admit that the only thing we can say absolutely about God's identity is it is always and forever absolute mystery so that whichever metaphors we use for God can never fully describe God. However, there are several elements of motherhood which allow the word mother to be a resonant, vibrant metaphor for God.

So far every human being on earth is born of a woman. Our mothers are the creative source of our lives who precede us and generate us. They are there before us and it is in their bodies that we take form and shape. God gives the possibility of creating new life to a man and a woman who together cause a life to begin, but then for nine months it is in the mother's body where the child lives and moves and has her being. The Apostle Paul used the analogy of pregnancy when he said, "In him we live and move and have our being (Acts 17:28). Just as the child has life in the mother, so we have life in God. God is like a mother.

Unlike many of God's nonhuman creatures, baby humans need to be nourished, protected and taught for many years by a mother or others who assume the mothering role. As a child grows up she associates her mother with the very primitive experiences of comfort, play, discovery, nurture, love and compassion, security in being held and sheltered. Increasingly, fathers are becoming more involved in mothering roles than in generations past. These parental activities are activities of God toward the children of God's womb. God is like a mother.

From the mother's point of view, mothering involves the creative activity of beginning life, giving birth, and providing for the child's growth, food first of all and then emotional and intellectual nourishment. It is the mother who feels the first stirrings of new life weeks before anyone else in the whole world knows that a miracle is happening in her body. Many women, especially during a first pregnancy, are so aware of what will be required of them in terms of the child's physical, mental and emotional growth that they ask themselves the question, "Am I capable of doing this?"

A woman can be hurt by what damages her child. There is such power in the delivery of new life and warmth and strength in freely given love that bears responsibility to rear what one has created that mothers are vulnerable to anything that hurts their children. The image of a doting, defenseless, sentimental woman as mother is not who we want to use in a metaphor about God as mother. Hosea 13:8 shows the power and wrath of God in feminine form: "I will fall upon them like a bear robbed of her cubs…" When God does get angry and is filled with wrath she can be pictured with feminine as well as masculine gender images. God is like a mother.

A mother's love, like God's, also extends way beyond her concern for her own children. The first known suggestion for a day set aside as Mother's Day was made by Julia Ward Howe in 1872.[8] Her idea was not that it should be a day when mothers are given lovely flowers and cards and served breakfast in bed, but rather a day when people should think about, pray and work for peace. The Civil War had ended just a few years before so this was to be a day when bereaved mothers and families could demonstrate their opposition to war and their determination to have warfare ended.

The relationship between mother and child connotes interdependence and mutuality of life at the deepest level, a quality of intimacy and familiarity that is genuinely person creating. Children who are neglected from their birth are described as "failure to thrive" children. The absence of touching and holding and being spoken to deprives these children not only of mental and emotional health but of physical health as well. A mother's love for her child nurtures the child into personhood. And the love of the child for the mother enriches the personhood of the mother. God is like a mother.

It is with these associations in mind that the relationship of mothering, when it is not restricted by the anthropological and sociological boundaries created by patriarchy, offers a wide range of excellent metaphors with which to name toward God the Creator. However, even as we try out the title "Mother" as a name for God we need to be careful not to sentimentalize motherhood lest we imply that motherhood is the highest, best and only calling of women. Speaking of God as

---

8.   This is not the only claim made for the origin of this holiday.

Mother gives us a new, authentic way to speak about God. Some people would argue that feminists are trying to change God by this new language about God. We are not changing God. We are changing, broadening and deepening our understanding of God and gaining new insights on how we should live in relation to God and to the world.

When we say, "God our Mother," we are describing the same Being whom we are accustomed to describing only in masculine terms. This Being is the One who is without beginning and without ending, who is totally free and who is absolute mystery. While for centuries this Being has been described as Father, the source of all being is also Mother. She gives life to all and she is the life of all. Like a mother, she freely gives herself to all creatures without expecting a return, but always hoping to be loved in return. She loves all her creatures inclusively, and joyfully affirms their value. This mother love makes us all brothers and sisters since we have all been carried in and born from the same womb, the womb of God our Mother. Like a mother, she is happy when the world flourishes, feels badly about the weaknesses of the world and pours forth her powerful love to resist all that damages her beloved creation.

The compassion of God the Mother shows us that she loves the weak and dispossessed as much as she does strong and powerful. While the world values those who have power and strength more than it does the weak and the dispossessed, each person has their own value in God's sight. This deep and abiding love does not need to be earned or deserved, because like a mother, God gives it freely and abundantly.

It is possible to turn this image of a mother's love into a namby-pamby love that is not strong and supportive, one that gives in to the whims of her children. However, there is also toughness inherent in mother love. Mothers have such a stake in the well-being of their children that they stand in judgment on whatever hurts their children. The process of gestation, birthing and feeding is not fully described with words that express tenderness, softness, pity or sentimentality. A metaphor of God as mother includes images of God our Mother as one who is not weak and passive, but as one who is strong and active in protecting her children.

God our Mother cares for the whole of creation, for all who live in her household. However, like a human mother she turns her attention in a special way to those most in need. Her will is for good life for all; therefore she wills justice for all, equal opportunity for all. Mothers in dangerous situations exemplify the self-giving love of Mother God. Like God, mothers do not conceive, birth and nurture children and then quietly watch as these children are brutalized in whatever way. They seek justice for their own children and for the children of other women.

The word justice is one of those English words that can be spoken and then interpreted with different meanings by different hearers. One way the word is understood is as an ethic of right, where what a person is called on to do in order to practice justice is to respect the rights of others while pursuing his or her own unalienable rights. In this definition a person is considered moral and just by simply doing no harm to others. The principle is that one must pursue their own well-being first and foremost to the extent that it does not harm someone else. It focuses on the just exercise within the law of individual rights.

Another way to understand justice is to see it as an ethic of care. In an ethic of care the emphasis is on a person's responsibility within a relationship rather than on a principle. Ethical judgments are based on one's understanding of effects on relationships rather than being based on principles. People who study female experience have found that a significant number of girls and adult women know moral principles as well as men and boys do, but they consider first and foremost the preservation of relationships; they put relationships above the principles.

In general discussions about ethics people think of these two as polar opposites. The ethic of rights has to do with the intellect deciding what is right and what is wrong. The ethic of care is, at heart, showing mercy. In feminist thought the two are not in opposition to each other. Mother God's compassion is an indispensable extension of her justice orientation. The compassion (womb-love) of God-Mother-Creator extends to her passion for justice. Instead of only passing judgment on others, as a king or monarch or judge would, God suffers with those who suffer.

> Maternity with its creativity, nurturing and warmth, its unbounded compassion and concern for justice, its sovereign power that protects, heals and liberates, its all-embracing immanence, and its recreative energy shapes a new understanding of divine relationality, mystery, and liberating intent.[9]

Using the image of mother makes real to us that we do abide in God as we did in our mother's womb and that God abides with us, knowing us better than we know ourselves. In our human experience we do not remain small children but grow into maturity that encompasses not only our origins with our mother but also becomes friendship and mutual help. All creatures, human and nonhuman,

---

9.   Johnson, *She Who Is,*185.

and the earth have their origin in God and exist in a relationship of friendship and mutual help to God who can be named Mother.

10

The Trinity

○ ○

...one Lord, one faith, one baptism, one God and Father of all, who is above all and through all and in all. (Eph 4:6)

The God of inexhaustible mystery who is inexpressibly other is also with the world in the flesh of history, and is furthermore closer to us than we are to ourselves. Sophia-God is beyond, with, and within the world; behind, with and ahead of us; above, alongside and around us. [1]

Every now and then I say something that I wish I hadn't said, something that maybe hurt someone's feelings or gave a false impression about someone or something. This seems to be common to most people's experience and usually the regrets fade away and are forgotten. But once in awhile I say something I remember and regret for years afterwards.

One such instance was about fifteen years ago when a friend who was beginning to be more attentive to her spiritual growth told me she was worried about her faith because she thought more about God than she did about Jesus. In fact, she worried because she gave Jesus such a minor role in her thinking and praying. I have regretted my answer to her many times in the intervening years because I told her that was a good sign inasmuch as it showed that her faith was a more mature faith. I answered as though believing in Jesus was childish and she was a good Christian for outgrowing such a faith.

Although I am expressing regrets here, the point of telling this story is not to cleanse my conscience but to illustrate that many of us have a real lack of under-

---

1.   Ibid., 191.

standing of the meaning of the Trinity. It is quite common for believers to be vague or confused about the persons of the Trinity and how they relate to each other and to us, but I am a seminary educated person and still I did not have enough of a grasp of the meaning of the Trinity to be able to answer my friend with a good, sound, helpful answer. The concept of one God in three persons may be at the top of the list of mysteries surrounding God. The neglect and misunderstanding of the Trinity which prevails today has been around since the beginning of Christianity.

Because we can't explain the Trinity we ignore it or diminish it, as I did in my answer to my friend. This lack of attention to the meaning of the Trinity—to the activity it describes—results in our misunderstanding God in two different ways. On the one hand, if we don't think of God in Trinitarian terms, God becomes a monolithic and monopersonal being who exhibits only the activities of a powerful God who rules his creation from on high separated from his creation. We know from our own personal experience that God is active in our lives and in history, but when we think of God only as one, almighty and separate, he becomes someone in the heavens who looks down upon his human creatures with approval or disapproval, intervening in worldly affairs with rewards and punishments. Viewing God's being in this way not only separates God from people but from the beauty and variety manifest in all parts of the creation God called good. When we view God only through this lens it is hard see her involved in her creation in the intimate ways we experience her. The question becomes: how can God be remote reigning from on high and still be part of our lives in intimate ways?

On the other hand, if we think of God as three separate persons apart from each other, as each one of us is a person separate from others, we find ourselves with another problem. This is the kind of thinking that inspired my answer to my friend. Not only did I see God as three separate persons, but as three separate persons arranged in a hierarchy: God is more important than Jesus; Jesus is more important than the Holy Spirit; the Holy Spirit is last in importance. I was saying it is desirable to outgrow Jesus and to hardly notice the Holy Spirit at all. However, the symbol of the Trinity is not meant to separate God into three gods of varying importance. Rather it is a revelation which shows us how God comes and goes in our lives. In the Trinity we see God as Creator, Redeemer, and Sustainer—activities which suggest to human beings that God is three in nature. God is not an isolated, ruling monarch, but rather an active being seeking relationship with her creatures. This dynamism is lost when we rely solely on the concept that God is one or on the concept that the persons of the Trinity are separate and are arranged in order of importance. Not only is the dynamism lost, but in a way we can end up with four gods instead of the One who is experienced in three ways. We are left with God Almighty and with God the Trinity.

Enough has already been said to make us want to shelve this impossible discussion and move on to something simpler. However, if we ignore the Trinity because it is too difficult to understand we deprive ourselves of an understanding of God which brings God, as a guide and as a friend, right into the midst of our daily lives. Faith is robbed of depth and richness when we fail to recognize the dynamic activity of God who moves not only as Creator but also as Redeemer and Sustainer—one God whose three roles are described as three persons.

From a feminist perspective there are two serious difficulties which accompany any discussion of the Trinity. One is the exclusive use of male imagery and the other is the hierarchy in which the three are placed. In most definitions of the Trinity there are clearly two male figures, a father and a son. The third figure, the Holy Spirit, is a more shadowy figure but is still usually referred to as "he".

Classical Trinitarian theology defines the three persons of the Godhead as being masculine. Consequently, that is the language and emphasis of our worship and our Christian education. This insistence on maleness for the Divine obscures the femaleness of God's image. It has the effect of casting men into the role of God and leaves for women the role of dependent and sinful humanity with no reflection in the image of God.

The ancient truth of the Trinity must be expressed in ways which will free God from the confines of masculinity to which Christianity assigned her, ways which will affirm the equality of male and female in the image of God. In the search for new ways of expressing ancient truth feminist theologians have proposed a variety of options: using both male and female imagery; using personal imagery without gender such as friend, redeemer; using nonpersonal terms which include biblical names such as Abba, Servant, Paraclete; retrieving the meaning of God the Father in a nonpatriarchal sense as Jesus used it. Names such as Creator, Redeemer, Sustainer, Paraclete raise images of masculinity because that is the gender which has always been attached to those words when speaking about God.

Besides addressing the difficulties presented by using only male images for the persons of the Trinity, feminist theologians have struggled with the traditional hierarchical order of the three persons. Classical descriptions of the Trinity state a progression of the three persons: God, Son, Spirit, while at the same time insisting that the three are equal. When Son and Spirit originate from the first person neither of them attain the authority of the Father, thereby becoming subordinates. We need to discover and learn to use different metaphors which show the relationship between the three as alive, vigorous and energetic, an active relationship that is one of equality, mutuality and reciprocity.

> First steps toward a feminist theological interpretation of Trinitarian language are taken when it is remembered that this symbol of holy mystery arises from the historical experience of salvation, and that it speaks about divine reality not literally but by way of analogy.[2]

The symbol of the Trinity developed historically out of the real life religious experience of people who saw this gracious God acting in their lives. The early expressions of the faith of the Jews and Gentiles who became Christians did not use the title "Trinity," but the stories they told, the songs they sang, the words of praise they raised were expressed in threefold symbols of God which arose spontaneously out of their experience as followers of the Way. The early Christians who were from Jewish backgrounds continued to speak of God as YHWH, the God of Israel, but now they had experienced God in Jesus Christ. He had touched their lives in ways which convinced them that he was Emmanuel, God with them. After Jesus, God in human form, was taken from them the power of the Holy Spirit came upon them in the form of wind and flame. This experience of the coming of the Holy Spirit sustained believers in their preaching and in giving their lives to God. They saw the One God in their lives in three ways.

As it was for them so it is for us. Our understanding of God corresponds to the way we have encountered the divine mystery in our daily lives. The way people find God in their lives, in their personal history and the history of the world points to three interrelated ways of being within God's own self. As we think about God our thinking has to move from the world, from where we are, to God. We can never think from God to the world because we are not God. We are not inside God's skin, so to speak.

Past descriptions, analogies for the Trinity, are helpful as we search for new ways to describe this mystery today. Metaphors which describe activity and life without a hint of maleness or hierarchy can be more inspiring to men and women alike. For example, Hildegaard of Bingen, a German mystic of the twelfth century, described the Trinity as a brightness, a flashing forth, and a fire. This illustration of something which is one, and yet three, is vivid and full of force. More recent theologians have described the Trinity in equally lively terms. Sallie McFague experiments with understanding God as mother, lover, and friend of the

---

2.   Ibid., 197.

world.[3] Elizabeth A. Johnson cites several expressions for the Trinity including Dorothy Sayers' which is a book, thought, written, and read.[4] All these metaphors for the Trinity reflect the livingness of God who is beyond, with and within the world.

Primarily following Elizabeth Johnson's thoughts through this discussion, as we have been doing, we speak now of the nature of the Trinity as transcending male or female. Because male and female are created equally in the image of God (Gen 1:26), we have said that each person of the Trinity may be spoken of in feminine terms. We have observed that Scripture and classical theology have helped move this discussion forward in the case of the individuals of the Trinity, but it becomes more difficult when we speak of the Trinity as a whole and the relationship between the three. In Christian history the portrayal of Father, Son and Holy Spirit has been overwhelmingly masculine. For the most part female imagery for the Trinity as a whole has been absent.

> It is not essential for the truth of God's triune mystery to speak always in the metaphors of father, son and spirit, although virtually exclusive use of these names over the centuries in liturgy, catechesis, and theology has caused this to be forgotten. At this point in the living tradition I believe we need a strong dose of explicitly female imagery to break the unconscious sway that male Trinitarian imagery holds over the imaginations of even the most sophisticated thinkers.[5]

The traditional Trinitarian names of Father, Son and Holy Spirit are suitably used when it is remembered that they are symbols or figures of divine relations but are not literally binding. Therefore, speaking from a perspective that values the equal humanity of women as being in the image of God, in the image of Christ and in the image of the Spirit, we are freed to use female nouns and pronouns as we try to speak about the unknowable.

When we talk from an explicitly feminist theological stance, it becomes clear that the central aspects of classical Trinitarian doctrine are strongly compatible with insights which are dear to the feminist theological perspective. The emphasis on relationship that is so typical of women is seen in the very essence of God which is to be in a relation of genuine mutuality. Speaking about God as three persons is speaking about a relationship.

---

3.   McFague, *Models of God*, (Philadelphia, Fortress,1987) 181.
4.   Johnson, *She Who Is*, 210.
5.   Ibid., 212.

Relation is the very principle of their being. No statement about one is true if taken in isolation from the other relations that equally constitute God's holy being. What this indicates in simple terms is that there is no absolute divine person. There are only the relative three: "They are always one in relation to the other and neither the one nor the other alone." At the heart of holy mystery is not monarchy but community; not an absolute rule, but a threefold *koinonia*[6]

A way out of the dilemma of referring to the Trinity in masculine or feminine language could be to call God "it." If God was an idol on a shelf we could use the word it, but God is a living being in relationship with us. God is active in our lives as the Creator of all that is, as the Redeemer who makes things right and as the Sustainer who is God's presence with us always. God is a personal God who relates to us the creatures and whose three persons relate to each other. Speaking of the relationship of the three persons lends itself very well to feminine imagery because relationship is woman's way of being in the world.

> Connectedness is intrinsic in female life, and certainly when we envision the Divine as female we release a new and unique emphasis on relationship…The world has not really tried divine love as Mother love. But when it does, divine love may break upon us with fresh and unexpected intimacy…[7]

In the words of a much beloved and perhaps trite Disney song, "what the world needs now is love, sweet love." The world needs the sweet love of God who values relationship like a divine Mother who would draw all humanity into her lap and make us into a global family, into a circle of persons who count one another as friends.

Friendship is a meaningful and valid analogy to use for the relatedness of the persons in the Trinity. Friendship is the freest, the least possessive, the most mutual of relationships, able to cross social barriers in genuine reciprocal respect. In friendship there is mutual trust in the reliability of the others. Friends are fundamentally side-by-side in common interests, common delights, shared responsibilities. Mature friendship is open to the inclusion of others thereby showing hospitality.

Classical theology hesitates to use the idea of friendship as a metaphor for the Divine out of fear of blurring the distinctions between the persons. But in

---

6. Ibid., 216.
7. Sue Monk Kidd, *The Dance of the Dissident Daughter,* (Harper San Francisco, 1996) 155.

healthy human friendship the stronger the bond between the friends the more creative of personhood the relationship is. Even in that strong bondedness friends are not interchangeable with one another nor are the persons of the Trinity interchangeable.

The metaphor of three women who are friends expresses the idea of the Trinity in a lively way. They are separate individuals, each with her own gifts and talents and purpose in life, but there is something that unites them with the loving bonds of friendship. The uniting factor(s) may be one or more of many things: the hobbies they enjoy, the friendship circles of their children or their husbands, the work of their church, the devotion to social justice causes. Whatever it is draws them together to share all kinds of experiences including talking and listening, working and playing, laughing and crying. In essence the three, even though separate individuals, are united in their love for and appreciation of each other. This kind of friendship is an apt analogy for the One Holy Wisdom consisting of three persons: the unreachable Abyss who embraces and befriends the world; the Word that became incarnate and the overflowing Spirit that seeks out the darkest, deadest places to bring new life. When we describe the Trinity using the metaphor of three women who are friends we are employing an alternative to the exclusive use of male images which is typical of classical theology and the hierarchical pattern that quite often, though subtly, accompanies it.

As we talk about how the persons of the Trinity are related to each other we must talk about the equality of the three. The idea of three women friends as a metaphor for the Trinity may present a problem because, in working so hard to meet needs of others, women tend to be unable to relate on an equal footing not only to men but to other women. Being this way, women can deny that they themselves have needs or they develop the feeling that no one else recognizes their needs. Both of these failings are exacerbated when women become so entrapped in caring for others that they are unable to cherish and nurture their own personhood.

Within the relationship that is the Trinity the three persons who are equal do not lose their distinctiveness and cannot be interchanged. Classical doctrine upholds this same feminist insight, that the relationship of the three is one of equality, even though the expressed progression of the three is Father, Son and Holy Spirit which is easily misunderstood as an order of importance.

The community of equals in the Trinitarian formula is the heart of a feminist vision of ultimate shalom: where differences exist, but are not arranged in a hierarchy and do not foster domination; where a relationship of bonding exists that helps persons to become subjects of history, not objects, because they are in community; where community will flourish through the practice of equality and relationship by its members. Basing our view of the world on the Trinity as a community of equals will weaken the idea that persons have a specific place in a line of command from top to bottom and that domination of some over others is ordained by God. The Trinity models the ideal sought by feminist thinkers.

In tending me as Grandma tended her violets God has used many seemingly little things to grow me. One of them is the song "We Are Climbing Jacob's Ladder," a favorite of mine from church camp. I always sang it with a good feeling that I was indeed climbing higher, getting closer to God. Then at a women's conference we sang the tune using the words, "We are dancing Sarah's circle." What an eye-opener! In that instant I felt a previously unknown appreciation for women and the way they embody relationship. Once again in these later years, God has used that song to change my understanding—now I can see that dancing Sarah's circle is a lively description for the life of the Godhead, the Three in One.

> ...a divine round dance modeled on the rhythmic, predictable motions of a country folk dance are one way to portray the mutual indwelling and encircling of God's holy mystery....Casting the metaphor in yet another direction, we can say that the eternal flow of life is stepped to the contagious rhythms of spicy salsas, meringues, calypsos or reggaes where dancers in free motion are yet bonded in the music.[8]

This lively description paints for us a picture of three distinct persons existing in each other in an enthusiastic movement of equal relations. Viewing the nature of God in this way is a model for human interaction that would produce respect and honor between people.

---

8.   Johnson, *She Who Is.*, 220.

11

One Living God: SHE WHO IS[1]

○ ○

So we know and believe the love God has for us. God is love, and those who abide in love abide in God, and God abides in them. (I John 4:16)

The one relational God, precisely in being utterly transcendent, not limited by any finite category, is capable of the most radical immanence, being intimately related to everything that exists. And the effect of divine drawing near and passing by is always to empower creatures toward life and well-being in the teeth of the antagonistic structures of reality. [2]

One of the delights of Grandma's violets was finding the newly forming buds hiding under the thick foliage of the violet plant. A tiny bud would be growing even as the stem which gave it nourishment grew and straightened, until the bud was upright and ready to open into full bloom. The realization of God's living presence in my life has been like that. In the thick foliage of my spiritual life, blossom bearing stems, appear and soon something new is budding there.

I have known God in my life since I was a child, but for a long time I thought about him being "up there" or "out there" somewhere. Jesus was the one I knew as person who was present in the world as a human being and who therefore knew my joys and struggles. Jesus, for me, was not primarily a person of the Trinity but a human companion teaching me how to live my life. I worshipped and prayed to God as a remote Being in heaven.

---

1.   Ibid., 224.
2.   Ibid., 229.

Slowly, like the budding of the violets, it began to dawn on me that the Tri-une God is involved in every facet of my life. An example of this early budding happened when I was asked to preach on the Bible and public policy at Sunday morning worship in a Lutheran church in Chicago. One of the positive sides of being a minister, but not being a pastor who has to write a sermon every week, was that I could have a sermon "brewing" in my mind for weeks and when the time came to write it all I needed was an outline. Sometimes the outline was more detailed than at other times but it usually amounted to two or three pages. That particular Saturday night, as I finished the outline for the next day's sermon, I had only one page. I stewed and fretted about the brevity of that outline and felt sure I would fail miserably the next morning. However, at that point in time in sermon preparation there is just one thing to do—leave it alone and pray hard.

The next morning during the service, just before the sermon, the pastor leaned over to me and whispered that he never preached from the pulpit. He always preached from the center aisle. When he suggested that I do that too, I was so thankful for having only one piece of paper in my left hand so that I could hold the microphone in my right hand. I knew with certainty that God had been present with me while I was writing the outline, giving me only as much as I needed for the occasion. This seems such a small thing for which to give God praise, but the same kind of things happen over and over again when I am in tune with God's presence living within me.

Praying to God, who is above and beyond all that is created was the way I had always prayed. This preaching event was among many events which happened and continue to happen which convince me that God is related to me and to the world in a very intimate way. Christian theology needs to recognize both the immanence and the transcendence of God because faith becomes lopsided and inadequate if one is emphasized more than the other. When transcendence is emphasized, God is seen only as a great power who may or may not respond to our most heartfelt prayers. To define God strictly as one who is so transcendent as to be unreachable is to make God irrelevant in the daily lives of people.

When I was taking a clinical pastoral education course in preparation for my ordination I spent time each day visiting patients who were newly admitted to the hospital. In the course of conversation with them, they would often express their confidence that God would heal them. Frequently, when I asked such folks where they worshipped, they replied that they didn't. For them there was a God in heaven who could be called upon to intervene in a crisis, but he was not part of their daily lives. He was, for them, totally transcendent.

On the other hand, when only the immanence of God is recognized, God can be made too small and treated too familiarly with words on bumper stickers and sayings on tee shirts. God and God's power can easily be trivialized.

The classical theologians wrote of God as Almighty, All Powerful, and All Knowing. Instead of starting with the activity of the Trinity who is known in relation to the world, they started with the idea of God as whole in himself and set apart from his creation. It can be argued that the result over the centuries has been that Christians have come to worship two divine beings: one who is set apart from and over all and one who is known in our lives as the Trinity. The description of the one God who is unmoved, unresponsive and solitary sets apart the divine being from his creation. The description of God as a Trinity describes God as three persons in relation to each other and to us—God who is living in the very life of all parts of her creation.

The image of God as standing alone in complete transcendence unaffected by the world has set up on the one hand the ultimate description of a man—strong, independent and in charge—and on the other hand has set the expected norms for how men should behave. Clearly, the idea of a transcendent God sets the stage for seeing God as a being who is alone, someone who doesn't need others in order to thrive. If this is how God is, so the reasoning goes, real men should be like that and thus we have a model for masculinity. Those who do not display these attributes are seen to be weak and ineffective, lesser beings. This logic leads to the attendant belief that being in relationship, which includes being vulnerable and at risk, is equivalent to being weak and ineffective.

> Thus it is not accidental that classical theism insists on a concept of God with no real relation to the world, even when this is interpreted as an affirmation of divine transcendence. Unrelated and unaffected by the world, such a theistic God limns the ultimate patriarchal ideal, the solitary, dominant male.[3]

However, there is another way for human beings to find themselves in relation to God. It is what might be called "woman's way of being." It is the way not of solitariness, but of relationship with others. It is a fullness of being that flourishes in genuine, two-way relations both with people who are alike and with people who are different.

> Women typically witness to deep patterns of affiliation and mutuality as constitutive of their existence and indeed of the very grain of existence itself. From

---

3.   Ibid., 225

this perspective the image of an unrelated or only superficially related God is a distortion.[4]

The importance of relating to others has led women to surrender themselves to the needs and desires of others to the point of denying their own needs and gifts. Because of her relationship to her husband, a woman will uproot herself from other important relationships to move far away to a strange place. Because of her relationship to her children she will work late into the night on something a child needs and then rise early to begin all over again to meet the needs of husband and children. It is easy and common for a woman to lose her own self identity as she tries to do what society expects of her in these relationships.

While a woman cherishes these precious connections she needs to know the importance of centering herself, affirming herself and choosing her own life's directions. Personhood for all, female or male, is not to be found in a self-sufficient ego, nor is it to be found in a self that is so diffuse as to have no being of its own. Selfhood needs to be based on a model that is both relational and autonomous. To talk about God from a perspective of women's experience points toward a relational God who loves freedom. Men and women alike are created to be free, to be individuals and at the same time to relate in wholesome ways to other people. This kind of naming toward God values names that glorify God as One who is above all and at the same time is in all and through all in her incredible, cherished creation.

Theologians, realizing from experience that God lives in the affairs of humans and in events in nonhuman creation, have described this relationship using the idea of the Trinity. Even though the naming came later in history, the Trinity existed from the beginning. The Trinity is not something to be added to the discussion after the One God is described. God was a Trinity from always. This description of God is the fellowship, the communion of Spirit, Son and Parent. The communion of the three persons makes up God's very essence. God is three persons in relationship with each other and with us.

We have said before the meaning of Sophia/Wisdom is the most developed personification of God's presence and activity in the Hebrew Scripture so that the very first Christians would naturally have associated Jesus with Sophia. Thus, we can appropriately name God in three ways: Spirit-Sophia, Jesus-Sophia, Holy Wisdom. We are looking at the persons not in the classical order, but in the order of Spirit, Incarnate Human, and Creator. Each of these persons has specific work.

---

4.   Ibid., 225.

Spirit-Sophia moves over the earth where she wills, bringing life and liberating power. She is the divine presence in all its wholeness. Jesus-Sophia brings the divine into the world as a particular person. He relates to all whom he meets, including the poor and the outcast, in order to demonstrate divine love. Holy Wisdom was in the beginning before anything else. She is the source and sustainer of all that is.

The fact that God does all of these things does not diminish the autonomous power of individuals—it does not make them into puppets. On the contrary God's creating and liberating power increase in direct proportion to one's communion, fellowship with the Trinity. God does not overshadow and overpower, but rather gives freedom. Nor does God intrude in the world occasionally to set things right. Rather, "God is in the world as ground, support, and goal of its historical struggling existence."[5]

Even though classical theology stresses the transcendence of God, it affirms, as does all Christian speech, that God dwells intimately in the world. However, an important question to raise is, "does the world dwell in God?" Three answers to that question are found in classical theism, in pantheism and in panentheism. Two of them answer "no," while one of them answers "yes." Classical theism maintains that the world exists outside of God. Theism's idea of God is that the Creator lives entirely apart from the created and, therefore, is not moved by what happens to the world and its peoples. If God did care for the world then God could be changed by the joys and sorrows of creation and, therefore, would be diminished. At the extreme opposite of this viewpoint is that of pantheism, in which God is the world and the world is God. God and the world are identical. In this view God is not a person; rather all aspects of creation are God. God ceases to be transcendent at all and merges with finite beings. There is no difference between God and the world so there is no way for true relation to exist.

Panentheism, the third viewpoint, answers "yes, the world does dwell in God." The simple little Greek word, *en*, makes all the difference. Pantheism, without the *en*, is a declared heresy because it takes away God's transcendence. But the word *en* means in and thus indicates that God is in everything and everything is in God. God dwells in the finite world, but God is more than the finite world. God's being is not completely swallowed up in the finite. Theism tends in the direction of transcendence, while pantheism leans in the direction of immanence. Panentheism displays both views in their full strength: God is transcendent and God is immanent.

---

5.   Ibid., 230.

To help us think about the idea of the world being in God, we could draw a circle to represent God, readily admitting that in so doing we are limiting God by the bounds of the circle. Within the circle, we could draw a smaller circle to represent the finite world. This simple diagram illustrates that God is in everything, but also that the world is in God.

If we accept this diagram as an authentic way of looking at God, we can see clearly that using images of motherhood for God is appropriate. God carries the world in herself, just as a female mother carries a child in her womb. An intriguing description of how this happens is found in the doctrine of the self-limitation of God which some Jewish philosophers of the Middle Ages formulated. It tells of God's special preparation for the creation of the world.

> In the beginning a dilemma exists because, since the infinite God is the fullness of being, boundless, there is no room for anything finite to exist. For the world to be possible at all some space must be hollowed out for finite being to exist in its own integrity, without being swallowed up by God's overwhelming infinity. In the act of creating, therefore, divinity withdraws. God makes room for creation by constricting divine presence and power. There is a contraction or concentration or infolding of the divine being in order to clear a space for the world to dwell. Into the resulting void shaped by divine self-limitation the creative word is spoken and the world is brought forth. Thus creation "outside" of God nevertheless remains "in" God, in the primordial space made possible by the self-contraction of the infinite. God's generous self-emptying is the condition for the possibility of finite existence in its own autonomy, while the difference between Creator and creature is embraced by the One who is all in all.[6]

Like a pregnant woman, God made a place, made room inside God for creation to exist. Every one of us has had our beginning inside the womb of a woman; a fact which should recommend the use of feminine metaphors for God. Exclusive use of male metaphors is unnatural because it is uniquely female to have room inside oneself for another. This view of God's relation to the world changes feelings about the bodiliness of women from those of disgust and abhorrence as found in classical Christian anthropology, to feelings of mysterious and generating love. If God is indeed like a mother, like a woman, then all the qualities of womanhood, made in the image of God, must be good and equal with those of manhood, made in the image of God, and thereby worthy of naming God. As with all metaphors, the one of a pregnant woman reaches its limits

---

6.   Ibid., 233.

because the time does come in the life of every human being when the baby separates from the mother's body.

Another analogy for the Divine that comes from panentheistic thought is friendship. Friends dwell within each other, in each other's hearts, minds and lives in ways that encourage each one to greater personhood.

> The better the friendship the more potent its capacity to generate creativity and hope, as experiences of trust, care, delight, forgiveness, and passion for common interests and ideas flow back and forth. In addition to its person-creating power, the love of mature friendship has the potential to press beyond its own circle to offer blessings to others. Befriending the brokenhearted, the poor, or the damaged earth with its threatened creatures are but some of the ways the strength of this relation can overflow.[7]

Not only does thinking of God as friend have a deep connection with women's experience of friendship, it is also in keeping with several key Bible verses. In John 15:12ff Jesus says,

> This is my commandment, that you love one another as I have loved you. No one has greater love than this, to lay down one's life for one's friends. You are my friends if you do what I command you. I do not call you servants any longer, because the servant does not know what the master is doing; but I have called you friends, because I have made known to you everything that I have heard from my Father.

John also quotes Jesus as saying, in essence, that those who are friends of Jesus are friends of God: "...that they may all be one; even as thou, Father, art in me, and I in thee, that they also may be in us, so that the world may believe that thou hast sent me" (Jn 17:21). When we become one with Christ we are one with God, even as Christ is one with God. We all become friends in a relationship of mutual love and care for one another and for the earth.

We have previously discussed the name, YHWH, which God gave to Moses at the burning bush. Moses was sure the people would ask who gave him such authority so he asked God what name he should give them in answer. The four consonants, YHWH, stand for the words with which God responded: "I AM WHO I AM" (Ex 3:14.) There are several ways to interpret this name.

For the Hebrew people God was too great for humans to pronounce his name. In Hebraic thought it was believed that a name is filled with mysterious power

---

7.   Ibid., 235.

and significance, for the name represents the innermost self or identity of a person. This is especially so with the name of God. Thus whenever they came to the letters YHWH in their reading of sacred text they would speak the word LORD. The very fact that they could not understand nor pronounce the name of God underlined for them and for us the deep mystery of who God is.

Another way to understand this name is to use it in a causative sense meaning that God causes whatever exists and whatever happens. Building on a likeness between the letters of the name and a Hebrew verb meaning "to be," we can understand the name to mean "I cause to be" or "I bring to pass." In Israel's faith the emphasis is upon the activity of the divine, not on a passive, eternal being. God assured Moses that Moses would know God by what he brings to pass. The answer to the question, "Who is God?" would be answered in events that would take place in the future.

Another interpretation of the name YHWH is "I shall be with you." God had asked Moses to do something so daring—facing and opposing the great and powerful pharaoh—that Moses felt totally inadequate. The very name YHWH brought reassurance and some measure of confidence to the reluctant man. The name promises that God will accompany people struggling under bitter oppression. God did then, and still does, accompany people who are struggling against the greed and cruelty of oppressive powers.

Of all the interpretations of the name given by God to Moses, the one that has had the strongest impact on theological tradition links the name with the metaphysical notion of being. YHWH means "I am who I am" or simply "I am" in a sense that identifies divine mystery with being itself. Many Bible scholars criticize this interpretation, saying that it is a philosophical understanding which is being read back into the original text. The Hebrew way of thinking was characterized by concreteness, not abstractness until it came in contact with Hellenistic culture. From the time the Hebrew scriptures were translated into Greek in a document called the Septuagint (sometime between 285-246 B.C.), the idea that YHWH describes God as being or essence, gained precedence in Jewish circles and was used widely in Christian thought.

Thus Thomas Aquinas is drawing on a long and honorable tradition when he uses the term "being" to refer to God. He believed that the divine essence is identical with divine existence. He finds this idea particularly suited to speaking of God because it refers to no particular aspect of God but rather to the whole. At the same time it underlines the uniqueness of God. Of no one else can it be said that their essence is to exist. Aquinas uses the phrase "HE WHO IS" as the most appropriate name for God.

In our corporate worship and in our private spirituality we are accustomed to thinking about names for God as masculine. This name, YHWH, is no different. Accepted English translations limit this phrase to the masculine. However, the original Latin of the name could be translated quite literally "who is" or "the one who is." The phrase in Latin has a masculine antecedent, *Deus,* but in keeping with our efforts to name toward God from a woman's perspective that honors women's dignity, Dr Johnson suggests a feminine gloss, a reading between the lines of this highly influential text, Exodus 3:14. In English the "who" is open to inclusive interpretation; it can be either female or male, thus providing an avenue for thinking about God in feminine terms. If women are truly created in the image of God, then when we say that God is "the one who is" we are freed to use the feminine for God and to say, "She Who Is."

> SHE WHO IS can be spoken as a robust, appropriate name for God. With this name we bring to bear in a female metaphor all the power carried in the ontological symbol of absolute, relational liveliness that energizes the world.[8]

The one who speaks from the burning bush is mystery but is at the same time personal and involved in the world.

> ...Symbolized by fire that does not destroy, this one will be known by the words and deeds of liberation and covenant that follow. SHE WHO IS, the one whose very nature is sheer aliveness, is the profoundly relational source of the being of the whole universe, still under historical threat. She is the freely overflowing wellspring of the energy of all creatures who flourish, and of the energy of all those who resist the absence of flourishing, both made possible by participating in her dynamic act. In the power of her being she causes to be. In the strength of her love she gives her name as the faithful promise always to be there amidst oppression to resist and bring forth.[9]

The mystery of God, Holy Wisdom, SHE WHO IS, is the presence of strong, enduring love in solidarity with the struggle of people to be free of abuse and oppression. The struggle to be free of words and actions that devalue them. The struggle to be free to accept their own dignity and value. Degradation, pain and suffering do not have the last word. They are encircled by the livingness of Sophia-God, who in the words of Paul, "gives life to the dead and calls into existence the things that do not exist" (Romans 4:17). She is the hope and gives the

---

8.   Ibid., 242.
9.   Ibid., 243.

hope that things will be better. Whenever and wherever good, loving things happen among human beings it is the Spirit of Sophia-God at work. Her name can be SHE WHO IS.

Not only does she bring into being good things, but as humans work with her they also take responsibility for the good of the world. As women and men are given life by SHE WHO IS, they in turn perform acts that are life-giving for their nearest neighbors and also for other humans who are in far distant places of the earth. Their love and care does not stop with human creation, but extends to the whole earth and all of its parts. All people who share the partnership of love with her have the power to change the forces that cause evil and suffering in the world which is the beloved creation of SHE WHO IS.

12

God Who Suffers

o o o o o o o o o o o o o o o o o o o o o o o o o o o o o o o o o
Whenever the LORD raised up judges for them, the LORD was with the judge, and he delivered them from the hand of their enemies all the days of the judge; for the LORD would be moved to pity by their groaning because of those who persecuted and oppressed them. (Judges 2:18)

In every generation women who work and suffer for justice's sake, withstanding the indifference or the rage of the powerful, are coworkers with the burning flame of Wisdom, sacraments of her liberating intent. Their lives are metaphor for the suffering engagement of the God who loves justice. [1]

"The devil owns my neighborhood. If I don't do something, God will not be here at all." These words of Hattie Williams, an African American woman who lived her whole life in the Oakwood/Kenwood area of Chicago, explained why she took the sufferings of her neighbors not only deeply in her heart but also squarely on her shoulders, doing what she could to alleviate their distress by fighting against the powers which had created and were sustaining the poverty there. Hattie's neighborhood included high rise public housing in which poor families by the thousands were stacked on top of each other in very poorly maintained eighteen story buildings.

It is now an area that is being gentrified with beautiful condos and single family homes, with stores and businesses. But during the sixties, seventies and eighties when Hattie's children and grandchildren were growing up, it was a place

---

1.   Ibid., 257.

where mostly African American people struggled to maintain their families. Employment was out of reach for most of these people because there were no businesses in the area and commuting to a job was difficult and time-consuming. Very few people could afford cars and the elevated trains had long since stopped serving the area. Hattie, who over the years received many local, state and national awards for her works of compassion, was dedicated to helping the people meet the everyday needs of their lives through helping them prepare for General Education Degree (GED) classes; teaching gardening, sewing, food preparation; holding self-esteem classes for young girls; leading classes in parenting; and sponsoring support groups for women. As a way of combating teen pregnancy she invited young black women who had succeeded outside the neighborhood to speak to younger girls about their lives and their hopes for success and happiness. She solicited food, clothing, furniture and money from churches and delivered these goods to people in the high rises. Her home, which was across the street from three of these high rise buildings, was the center for all this activity.

Her reach went far beyond the neighborhood, as she made friends with and taught white folks from suburban churches about the love and presence of God in their lives and in the lives of the people in the ghetto. Much of her teaching was done by encouraging people not only to give generously but to come to the neighborhood and meet the families they were helping. She risked political action against the powers of oppression wherever and whenever it might produce good results. Her whole life of service was based on prayer. On my spiritual journey the example she set was some of the most nutritious food that God fed me just as my Grandmother fed her violets to help them grow.

In the book of Judges we read:

> Whenever the LORD raised up judges for them, the LORD was with the judge, and he delivered them from the hand of their enemies all the days of the judge; for the LORD would be moved to pity by their groaning because of those who persecuted and oppressed them." (Judg 2:18)

God saw the misery of the people in the Oakwood/Kenwood area of Chicago and was moved to pity for them so she raised up Hattie to lead them. For some Christians the words "moved to pity," even though they are words from the Bible, convey an idea about God that is unacceptable to them because they believe that God cannot be moved, that God is unchangeable. For these people the Lord God Almighty, Creator of the Universe and all that is in it, does not feel pity. For them God must be unmoved in power and might, a ruler who never changes. For them God even causes suffering and pain as punishment or as a means of teaching people a lesson, all in the interest of their eternal salvation.

When I was working toward ordination one of the requirements of the Presbyterian Church (USA) was that I take a six month clinical pastoral education course at a hospital. Besides the classroom learning, I served as a chaplain in the wards of the hospital. One afternoon I was called to the oncology unit to be with the family of a young father who had just died. He had been dying from cancer for many weeks during which time his family and church friends had spent hours standing around his bed praying and singing. Throughout this whole time they told his twelve-year-old son and ten-year-old daughter that their dad was not going to die, that God was going to heal him, and that he would come home to be with them again. When he did die, they told the children not to cry because it wasn't sad, it was glorious. It was glorious because, they said, Jesus needed their dad in heaven. It is hard to accept the idea that a God who loves human beings would, to satisfy a selfish need, take away from children their loving father. It seems out of character for God who loves children to have more need for their father than do the children. What quite possibly would have offered real consolation to the children and brought them closer to God was to have said that Jesus was crying with them as he felt their grief at losing their father.

This family and its church, who believed that God Almighty is the cause of everything, would never have accepted the idea that God could suffer with them. Even though their theology would not be defined as classical theism they held the same belief in the matter of God suffering. Classical theism holds that God cannot suffer, so language that hints that God suffers has been barred for several reasons that are high-sounding and noble. One is that since suffering is punishment for sin, God cannot suffer because he is sinless and therefore not subject to the punishment of suffering.

Still another reason people think God cannot suffer or feel compassion is that pain and suffering are seen as an imperfection which is a result of one's own deficiency. For them suffering is incompatible with the greatness of God who is the source of all perfection and, therefore, can have no deficiency. Having compassion for the suffering of creatures would indicate that God's mood, so to speak, is dependent upon what is happening to God's creatures. In this view God is completely incapable of being changed by outside forces.

When you add to these ideas the belief that God is omnipotent you reinforce belief in the apathy of God. If God is omnipotent, in control of everything that happens, then while he may be benevolent he is still the cause not only of all good that happens but also of all evil. The attempt to explain how a good God could cause evil is a difficult and inexhaustible discussion which is much attempted. A commonly given answer to this dilemma has been that since destructive events do happen it must be God does not actually will them but rather he permits them to happen for some reason. In the case of the children whose father died from cancer, the reason for God allowing their father to die, would be that God needed him in heaven. Since God chooses not to prevent disasters, personal and communal, it must be that he has a good reason to allow them.

Some of the reasons given for suffering are that it punishes wrongdoing, tests character, educates, forms personality or brings forth a greater good. These are answers which human beings for generations have been giving to the question of why bad things happen to good people. In the face of deep suffering each one of us has, at one time or another, taken hold of one of these ideas for comfort.

In summary of the view of God as unmoved by suffering, we can say that since God is in control everything which happens does so because God wills it. Therefore, God would feel no sorrow or pity at something happening to the created world. For God's own purposes, God does not feel the pain of people all over the world who live in conditions similar to those in Hattie Williams' old neighborhood or in the many situations of hunger, poverty and war that exist in the world today.

The advent of instant communication has brought the terrible suffering of the world's people right into our own homes. We saw over and over again the suffering of the people at "Ground Zero" on and after 9/11. Even though the Iraqi war has been declared over we still see and hear reports of the suffering and death of military personnel and of the Iraqi people. We see and hear about the hatred, destruction and grief that accompany the politics of Israel and Palestine. We see and hear about the devastation wreaked daily on the African people by poverty, war and by HIV/AIDS. We see and hear about women and children all over the world who are victims of domestic abuse. We see and hear about the disappearance of people in Central and Latin American countries because of conflict between governments and rebel groups.

Fear of possible terrorist activity on our own soil since the attack on 9/11 is heightened by the security alerts broadcast by our government. The definition of terrorist is usually limited to those judged to be a threat to the USA or to the allies of our country. However, our definition of terrorist should include men who rape and abuse women and children, parents who abuse their children, lawmakers and citizens who attack and demean immigrants to this country or any other, nations that make war against other nations for reasons of self-interest, and the list goes on. The list of actions that should be called terrorist is long because terrorism exists in many forms. If God is a good and loving God, and I believe she is, she cannot be insensitive and uncaring about all this suffering and never, ever would she be the cause of it!

In the face of the radical suffering of so many millions of people in the world, the doctrine of the omnipotence of God would still tell us that God is causing it all and that it is okay because God sees his plan unfolding. However, this explanation of evil fails to satisfy the heartfelt questions of people everywhere.

> The idea of God simply cannot remain unaffected by the basic datum of so much suffering and death. Nor can it tolerate the kind of divine complicity in evil that happens when divine power is conceived as the force that could stop all of this but simply chooses not to, for whatever reason. A God who is not in some way affected by such pain is not really worthy of human love and praise. A God who is simply a spectator at all of this suffering, who even "permits" it, falls short of the modicum of decency expected even at the human level. Such a God is morally intolerable.[2]

An atheistic view is understandable, and maybe even called for, as a protest to the idea that a good God would stand by and watch, in some sense approving the suffering of his beloved creatures. Most human beings are deeply touched by tragedy. What kind of a God would not also be touched deeply by suffering? Atheists are not the only ones to raise the question of how God can stand above and watch all this. Some of the most creative theological thinkers of the contemporary times do so as well.

Protestant theology typically looks at the cross and talks about the genuine involvement of the Triune God in the pain of Jesus on the cross. God shares the pain in such a way that people are led to salvation. European Catholic thinkers say that the union of the divine and the human natures in Christ is so profound that it is not only the human Jesus who suffers on the cross, but also the divine Christ. Liberation theologians of South America teach that God is not only in solidarity with Jesus on the cross but is in solidarity with all the suffering people of the world.

Alongside the sufferings of people impacted by illness and accident, there are millions who suffer because of the prevailing idea that some people, religions, and nations have *the* truth and other people believe in lies. Even as the United States was dropping bombs on Afghanistan and then Iraq, officials talked about military action against other countries in the region that are considered, by some in our government, to be terrorist nations. It seems that most officials and many citizens of

---

2.   Ibid., 249.

the United States never give thought to the possibility that our great nation might also cause terror for others. Some people in the U.S. believe that God is on our side and that the good we claim to represent must win. The nations we consider our enemies feel the same about the God in whom they believe. Militant language from both sides sounds the same. The suffering of people caught in the middle of the struggle for control is minimized by the belief that judging another to be evil and winning the battle against that evil supersedes all other considerations.

Impassability is the word used for the doctrine that God cannot suffer the way his creatures do. However, this doctrine leaves open the possibility that God does suffer in a way that is appropriate for God. This idea as classically stated points to the mystery of God. Within the concept of the mystery of God there is room for new, creative ways of speaking about the suffering of God. Viewing the suffering of God from a feminist perspective brings new understanding of how God does suffer with her creatures.

Every era in the history of the world has had great suffering, but now is the time to understand that God is a suffering God. At this time in history, to say that God is untouched by human suffering is not a compliment to God but rather an expression of deficiency in God. Many of us have accepted the idea that God cares what happens to us. However, because of the power of patriarchy we have not been able to express that feeling in metaphors that come from the lives of women around us—our mothers, grandmothers, aunts, sisters and friends. We have not been free to see that God is like the mothers who lay down their own lives for the sake not only of their own children but also for the children of other mothers.

Language from a feminine perspective adds further precision to the idea of God who suffers with those she loves. Feminine metaphors are very meaningful and strong ways to describe the suffering and pain of God. Dr. Johnson sets forth four experiences which are common to women and which provide suitable ways for naming toward God. They are birth, justice and anger, grief, and degradation. The first two are activities which are creative in nature and are expressions of women's role in creating life and in protecting that life. The last two are situations where women face utter darkness and there is no way to explain the suffering in an understandable way. We shall take a closer look at each of them.

The first experience of women that provides suitable ways of naming toward God is that of giving birth in which a woman goes through suffering and pain of a kind that a man, or a woman who has not delivered a child, cannot imagine. In the Christian world that suffering was discounted for generations because Genesis states that women will have pain in childbirth as punishment for their sin in the Garden of Eden. Mercy Amba Oduyoye, an African feminist theologian, shines new light on that suffering when she likens it to the glory on the battlefield which patriarchy holds so dear. She says that when she was sixteen she watched an eighteen year old girl having her first baby. From that experience, Mercy knew why a woman of her tribe was said to have returned safely from the battlefield when she had successfully delivered her baby.

In the sixth century before Christ, the prophet Isaiah used the image of giving birth to describe God as the creator of new things. The Israelites were living in exile in Babylon in what they saw as punishment for their having turned away from the one true God. A hymn of creation, found in Isaiah, celebrates the old that God created and the new that God is creating. Such creating is a chaotic, painful process which this passage fittingly compared with giving birth.

> For a long time I have held my peace, I have kept still and restrained myself;
> now I will cry out like a woman in labor, I will gasp and pant. (Is 42:14)

The second experience of women that provides suitable ways of speaking of God in feminine terms is that of justice and anger. If we can let go of our masculine-only metaphors we will be freed to see in Isaiah's imagery of a woman giving birth the likeness of God as she who labors and strains to bring forth justice. God cries out in suffering as she pushes to provide lives of equality and fulfillment to all her human creatures. When those who are suffering cry out in pain, it is first the cry of God. That cry goes out to the people of God, whether suffering or not, and they are moved to seek justice for all.

Women suffer great risk when they engage in the struggle to secure justice for those who are oppressed. Through all the generations, and within our life time, there are countless numbers of women who have struggled at great risk for the justice for others. In 1956 twenty thousand South African women risked their lives by marching on government buildings. Peaceful but defiant, they protested the hated pass laws. After their silent protest they left singing: "You have struck a rock; you have tampered with the women; you shall be destroyed."[3] This is one example out of thousands of women in countries all over the world who run the same risks in response to the cries of suffering people. Self sacrifice is an activity of Sophia-God that can be named authentically from female experience.

> In every generation women who work and suffer for justice's sake, withstand-
> ing the indifference or the rage of the powerful, are coworkers with the burn-

---

3.   Ibid., 256.

ing flame of Wisdom, sacraments of her liberating intent. Their lives are metaphor for the suffering engagement of the God who loves justice.[4]

Anger goes hand in hand with seeking justice. As anger rises up in women against the injustices they and others suffer, it is not an anger that punishes. Rather, it is an anger that seeks to change things and gives energy to act and to resist. The prophet Hosea portrays this anger as that of a mother bear who has been robbed of her cubs, an anger that blazes and attacks (Hosea 13:8). This kind of anger bears witness to God's wrath which is prompted by a love for her beloved human beings that is deeper than we can even imagine. We tend to ignore or make excuses for the exploitation of the poor but in the heart of She Who Is their suffering is towering and devastating injustice

The two actions just described, birth and justice/anger, result in creative power. The next two actions, grief and degradation, are created by systemic injustice, historical chaos and personal wrongdoing all of which are damaging to humans deep inside their beings. Women's relational way of being opens the door to suffering, because we are so deeply related to those we love that their suffering is our suffering. The closeness to and love of the ones dear to her causes a woman to grieve when those loved ones are hurt in any way.

This desolation provides another reference point for speaking about God who also grieves over the evil done to her children. The Hebrew Scriptures are full of songs of sorrow and lament. Jeremiah, in 31:15-17, describes the devastation of Rachel as she weeps over the death of her children. In Isaiah 16:9, God laments the war that has devastated the orchards and fields. And again in Jeremiah God cries for those who are enemies of Judah (48:31,36).

The knowledge that God grieves at sickness, suffering, death and injustice gives women hope and strengthens them to resist in situations of danger.

> Weeping women, women whose hearts moan like a flute because those they love have come to harm, are everywhere in the world. As *imago dei* they point to the mystery of divine sorrow, of an unimaginable compassionate God who suffers with beloved creation. Holy Wisdom keeps vigil through endless hours of pain while her grief awakens protest. The power of this divine symbol works not just to console those who are suffering, but to strengthen those bowed by sorrow to hope and resist. If God grieves with them in the middle of disaster, then there may yet be a way forward.[5]

---

4. Ibid., 257.
5. Ibid., 260.

Women suffer physical, psychological and social degradation daily because they are female in a patriarchal world, a world that honors maleness above all else. This honoring gives males "permission" to control, rape, beat and abuse women, children and nature. They may escape censure and at times may even be commended by powers which seem to be sanctioned by a male God. Examples of women violated and left with no one to comfort or help them can be lifted up from the stories of every generation. In the Old Testament we read of Hagar being exiled into the desert with her young son (Gen 21:9-20), the princess Tamar being raped (II Sam 13), the young daughter of Jephthah being sacrificed even though she was beloved by her father (Judg 11:29-40), and the nameless concubine from Bethlehem who, with the encouragement of her master, was gang raped (Judg 9). In three out of these four biblical stories there is no criticism of the men who caused the suffering of the women.

There is a real sense in which the way women have been abused and tortured over the generations could be called a holocaust of women without diminishing the suffering of six million Jews in the Nazi death camps. We could tell horror stories of the treatment of women during the Inquisition, women during the Salem witch trials, women in Nicaragua, women in any country where there is warfare, and women on the streets of America's cities.

A current and very disturbing example is the torture of women in the Democratic Republic of the Congo. Since 1998, rebels have been attacking government forces and civilians with the aid of the countries of Uganda and Rwanda. Gang-rape has been so systematic, and so common in eastern Congo during this war that thousands of women are suffering from vaginal injuries which leave them torn and mutilated for the rest of their lives. Rape victims are commonly ostracized by their husbands and families, left with no emotional or physical support. The doctors in Congo now consider the destruction of the vagina to be a war injury and therefore a crime of combat.

War crimes against women are not unique to the Democratic Republic of Congo. Even a quick look at the topic on the web delivers more examples than one can handle emotionally. Among them are the 200,000 "comfort" women the Japanese army enslaved during WWII, and the women and girls who were gang raped by Bosnian Serb soldiers during the Bosnia Herzegovina conflict.

The tortured Son of God, on a rude cross, is for Christians the classic symbol of divine involvement in the pain of the world. Here was a man who put his ministry of love and healing before his own life; a man who committed no evil against anyone; a man who sought only to bring goodness and wholeness into a broken world. Here was God in human form, tortured and crucified, participating fully in the suffering of the world. Jesus Christ shows us that God does suffer and feel sorrow for the pain of all people. This symbol of God's active suffering includes the suffering lives of women and men of all ages.

> The suffering body of Christ includes the raped and denigrated bodies of women. As Asian theologian Virginia Fabella writes, all over the world desperately poor women "are today the Christ disfigured in his passion." It is a suffering that should not be.[6]

In our naming toward God, when we pay attention to women's experience of suffering and their response to suffering, we are compelled to use new names for God which present fresh and hope-filled ways for us to understand how God relates to us. Thinking of women in terms of their regard for relationship and their compassion gives us an avenue to understand how the God of love is active in the situations of pain and suffering being played out on the world stage today. One caution, however, is that it is destructive of human life to glorify suffering for suffering's sake. The idea that suffering should be welcomed because it is God's will is one of the tools of oppression so widely used. But God's empowering love is released when suffering is set in the context of the presence of God who is so utterly and completely committed to human beings that she suffers along with them.

God is love and with love comes suffering. In the light of women's experience, love includes such openness to the loved ones that one becomes vulnerable to all that hurts them, that one rejoices in their joys and grieves in their sorrows. God suffers with us just as we suffer with our children and with others in pain in the world. God suffers willingly because it is in her nature to love deliberately and generously. To think of God only as one who dwells above all the turmoil of the world as an impassive onlooker or angry judge is of no help to a suffering world. The reality of God who has suffered and is suffering with us is of enormous help and leads to hope as we live in this world. Knowing that we are not abandoned in our desperation makes it possible to survive whatever we face.

> This is because we are speaking about *God,* than whose power of love nothing greater can be conceived. If there be God, then there are parameters to evil, and a terminus. The human struggle can go forward in hard-won hope against hope that the compassion of God will overcome chaos and death and set limits even to the unfathomable mystery of evil. Speech about the suffering God

---

6.   Ibid., 264.

points forward: in the end all will be well, and so energy to resist despair arises.[7]

As we speak of God's suffering we are not trying to invent a literal description of God. The rules of metaphor apply here just as they do with masculine descriptions of the divine. The point of discussing the suffering of God is not to work out an intellectual system that would explain the mystery of God, but rather the point is that such discussion breeds hope. The result is that there is a wide arena where people of good will can act toward overcoming the evil that kills human dignity. Here and there, now and then, the actions of people of good will succeed in changing conditions of suffering.

> Against the background of the history of human injustice and suffering, the suffering God is a most productive and critical symbol for it cannot be uttered without human beings hearing the challenge to solidarity and hope...Speaking about the suffering of God, consequently, is a companion to criticism of those conditions that dishonor women, and indeed all human beings and living creatures. Even then it is valid only if accompanied by the struggle to change the conditions in the direction of a new heaven and a new earth.[8]

The recognition that God suffers calls believers to act against the causes of suffering of any of God's people whoever and wherever they may be. The action required goes beyond criticism of the evil and manifests itself in solidarity with the sufferers. The conditions that cause suffering must be challenged and changed. In this kind of fierce and demanding protest hope for the end of suffering is born. Movement against injustice transforms people and bonds them with one another and to the world after the manner of relationality. It is love binding people together to stand against the forces of suffering and death.

Light dawns, courage is renewed, tears are wiped away, a new moment of life arises. Toward that end, speaking about suffering Sophia-God of powerful compassionate love serves as an ally of resistance and a wellspring of hope. But it does so under the rule of darkness and a broken world.[9]

Nothing we can say about God will ever be adequate to describe the burning mystery which is the Divine. But opening up our vocabulary to include feminine

---

7.   Ibid., 268.
8.   Ibid., 271
9.   Ibid., 272.

names and pronouns will bring a dimension to our understanding of God which has been tragically neglected. The idea of SHE WHO IS brings to bear all the loving, care-giving, wisdom-supplying richness of the female created in God's image. The feminine in God is a reality we must accept if justice for all is to prevail in the world. ***We must learn a new language!***

List of References

Aldredge-Clanton, Jann, *In Search of the Christ-Sophia, An Inclusive Christology for Liberating Christians,* Mystic, CT.:Twenty-Third Publications, 1995.

Anderson, Bernhard W., *Understanding the Old Testament,* Englewood Cliffs, NJ: Prentice-Hall, 1957.

Armitage, Susan and Jameson, Elizabeth, eds., *The Women's West,* Norman and London: University of Oklahoma, 1987.

Bechtel, Carol, *Hallelujah: the Bible and Handel's Messiah,* Pittsburgh: *the* Kerygma program, 1995.

Carmody, Denise Lardner, *Biblical Woman: Contemporary Reflections on Scriptural Texts,* NY: Crossroad, 1992.

Clifford, Anne M., *Introducing Feminist Theology,* NY: Orbis, 2002.

Constitution of the Presbyterian Church (USA), Part 1 *Book of Confessions.*

Daly, Mary, *Beyond God the Father: Toward a Philosophy of Women's Liberation,* Boston: Beacon, 1973.

Fox, Matthew, *One River, Many Wells,* New York: Jeremy P.Tarcher, Putnam, 2000.

Gray, Elizabeth Dodson, *Sunday School Manifesto: In the Image of Her?* Wellesly, MS: Roundtable Press, 1994.

Johnson, Elizabeth A., *Consider Jesus, Waves of Renewal in Christology,* NY: Crossroad, 2000.

————, *She Who Is: The Mystery of God in Feminist Discourse,* NewYork: Crossroad, 1996.

Kidd, Sue Monk, *The Dance of the Dissident Daughter,* San Francisco: Harper, 1996.

Manley, James K., *Spirit, The Presbyterian Hymnal,* Louisville KY: Westminster/John Knox Press, 1990.

McFague, Sallie, *Metaphorical Theology, Models of God in Religious Language,* Philadelphia: Fortress, 1982.

———, *Models of God, Theology for an Ecological, Nuclear Age,* Philadelphia: Fortress, 1987.

Miles, Jack, *God, a Biography,* New York: Vintage, 1996.

Mitchell, Margaret, *Gone With the Wind,* Macmillan, 1945.

Newsom, Carol A. and Ringe, Sharon H., eds., The *Women's Bible Commentary,* Louisville: Westminster/John Knox, 1992.

Pagels, Elaine, *Adam, Eve, and the Serpent,* New York: Random House, 1988

Ruether, Rosemary Radford, *Women* and *Redemption, a theological history,* Minneapolis: Fortress, 1998.

Trible, Phyllis, *God and the Rhetoric of Sexuality,* Philadelphia: Fortress Press, 1978.

Van Wijk-Bos, Johanna W.H., *Reimaging God,* the *Case for Scriptural Diversity,* Louisville, KY: John Knox Press, 1995.

Webster's Mew *World Dictionary, Second College Edition,* NY: Simon and Schuster, 1980.

Winter, Miriam Therese, *WomanPrayer, WomanSong,* Bloomington, IN: Meyer-Stone Books, 1987.

978-0-595-36774-0
0-595-36774-7

Printed in the United States
148287LV00006B/5/A

9 780595 367740